GW00601281

Table of contents

Introduction

MANAGEMENT AND PLANNING

Money 98 is a good deal more than just a personal accounting program. It is a serious tool for the management of income, spending and assets, but a tool which combines user-friendliness, power and simplicity.

Money 98 can be used without any previous knowledge of accounting. All it takes is a little application and the steady learning of each function, and you will quickly be able to enjoy its benefits so that you are no longer navigating without instrumentation in the management of your personal finances. Money 98 is a comprehensive tool, enabling you to record all bank transactions, transfers, etc. and to break down any item of income or expenditure such as VAT, capital or interest on a loan. Money 98 is far more flexible than many other accounting programs; any entry can be amended or updated – for example, when a forecast expenditure becomes actual.

Money 98 offers a wide range of accounting and graphical presentations which make the analysis of the state of your finances clear and simple: reports, tables, graphs, pie-charts, and so on.

In Money 98, all movements of funds are classed in categories and subcategories, so that at any moment, Money 98 can supply you with information on account balances and due dates for regular payments. It also allows you to plan regular expenses, simulate different loan or savings scenarios and monitor investments in stocks and shares. And to make it even easier to gather the necessary accounting information, Money 98 integrates with online data services – accessible via the Internet – provided by your bank or by stock-market information services.

THE PURPOSE OF THIS BOOK

This book is not a substitute for the documentation supplied with Money 98 (user's manual, Help file and interactive tour) but is a guide to help you familiarise yourself with the various tools of the program and put them quickly into practice.

Follow each hour by applying the examples to your own data. In this way, you will be able to set up a system for managing your finances and assets. If you make a mistake, you can easily correct it and adjust your accounting model to fit the actual situation.

Even if some hours are not applicable to your situation, you should nevertheless take the time to consult them briefly. You will find elements which may prove useful later on if you want to develop your financial management. The book's division into twelve hours enables you to grasp all the functions of Money 98 as fully as possible.

CONVENTIONS

Throughout this book, you will come across various text panels.

These notes provide additional information about the subject concerned.

These notes indicate a variety of shortcuts: keyboard shortcuts, 'Wizard' options, techniques for experts, etc.

These notes warn you of the risks associated with a particular action and, where necessary, show you how to avoid any pitfalls.

Hour 1

Installation and getting started

THE CONTENTS FOR THIS HOUR

- Installing and uninstalling Money 98

- Starting Money 98

- Getting help in Money 98

This first hour deals with installing Money 98 and familiarising yourself with its Help and information search functions.

INSTALLING AND UNINSTALLING
MONEY 98

Money 98 is easily installed from the CD-ROM in Windows 95:

1. Place the CD-ROM in your CD-ROM drive. The Autorun process starts the installation program automatically (see Figure 1.1).

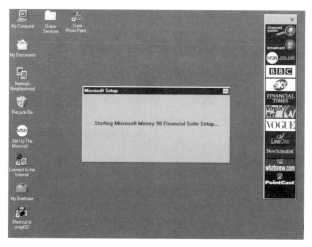

Figure 1.1: The installation program starts as soon as the CD-ROM is inserted

2. The installation program looks for any components already installed. Next, the program requests the user's identity. Enter your name. This name will be used for all subsequent installations of Money 98 or any of its components (see Figure 1.2).

3. The installation program proceeds to display the product serial number. Click on **OK** to continue with the installation.

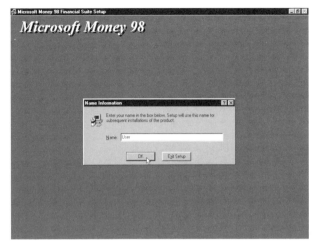

Figure 1.2: Window for entering the name of the user

4. The installation program indicates the destination folder, i.e. the location where Money 98 will be installed. If the default location is not suitable, change it by clicking on **Change Folder** (see Figure 1.3).

5. Click on the **Money 98** icon to confirm the installation. The program begins copying files. This phase takes some time, but an indicator shows you the progress of the installation. When all files have been copied, the installation program asks whether you want to use Online Banking services. Click on **No** if you do not have a modem or if you do not want to use these services. Click on **Yes** if you have a modem and want to use these services.

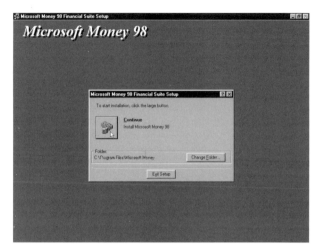

Figure 1.3: Money 98 will be installed in the default folder or any other folder specified by the user

Online banking services are offered by many banks and financial institutions. With Money 98, you can automatically download data from these services for integration with your own data, e.g. bank statements, stock-market prices, etc.

6. The Money 98 installation process finishes with a screen offering a tour of Money 98. This gives you an interactive tour of the product and its main functions (see Figure 1.4). Run the tour if you would like to see a summary of its features.

To uninstall Money 98, run the installation program again and select the **Uninstall** option. You should not uninstall the program unless you no longer want to use it or you want to transfer it to another disk or another computer.

Uninstalling Money 98 does not destroy the files created since the program was installed, nor the backup copies of these files. If you reinstall Money 98 after uninstalling, you will be able to continue using these files. If Money 98 is reinstalled to a different directory and/or disk from that used for the previous installation, you will need to move these files manually to the new location.

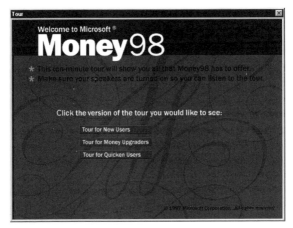

Figure 1.4: Tour menu

STARTING MONEY 98

After installation, Money 98 is launched from Windows 95 by selecting it from the Windows 95 Taskbar. If a shortcut has been created on the Windows 95 desktop, click on the corresponding icon. The Money 98 Home screen provides access to the various functions of the program.

■■■■■ Function bar and Navigation bar

The first time Money 98 is started, the Tour screen is displayed (see Figure 1.4). Once an account has been created, the Home screen will be displayed, showing information about this account (see Figure 1.5). The upper bar gives access to the functions of Money 98:

- **File.** Create a New File, Backup, Archive, Import, Export, Print Setup, Print, Exit Money 98.

- **Edit.** Undo, Cut, Copy, Paste.

- **Go.** Back, Money Home, Accounts, Bills, Online Banking, Investments, Planner, Money Insider, Categories.

- **Favorites.** Add to Favorites, Favorite Accounts, Favorite Reports.

- **Tools.** Find, Update Internet Information, Payees List, Categories List, Calculator, Options.

- **Help.** Access to online Help. For example, you can start the Money 98 Tour if you did not run it when you first used the program.

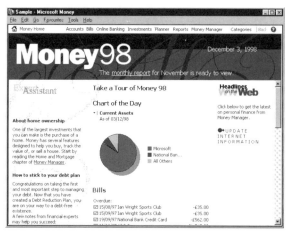

Figure 1.5: Money 98 Home screen for an existing managed account

The second bar enables you to move between the various headings offered under Go on the upper bar. The remainder of the screen shows various items of information relating to the account currently in use (see Figure 1.5):

- **Assistant.** This is a short text offering information about a function of Money 98 which has not yet been discovered or used.

- **Chart of the Day.** This is a chart chosen at random from various possible graphics, providing a visual representation of the state of your accounts and assets.

- **Bills.** This is a list summarising all items of income and expenditure due for receipt or payment. The account balance is shown at the bottom of this list.

- **Headlines on the Web.** These headings are only relevant if you have a modem and Internet access. They provide access to online information services.

GETTING HELP IN MONEY 98

You can access the Money 98 online Help file at any time. Several levels of help are available:

- **General help.** Click on the question mark at the right-hand end of the Navigation bar (red circle) or the question mark on the Function bar (see Figure 1.6), then click on **Help Topics**. Another option, marked **Help for Quicken Users**, is specially designed for users of Quicken, and explains the procedures to be followed to convert their data files in Quicken format for use in Money 98.

- **Context-sensitive help.** To get help on a particular item, right-click on the item concerned, then click on the button marked **What's This?** Alternatively, click on a field and then press **F1** (see Figure 1.7).

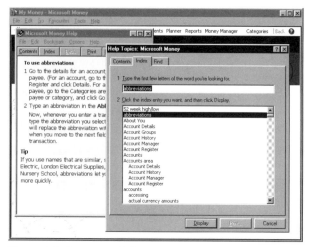

Figure 1.6: Access to Help and the Help Index

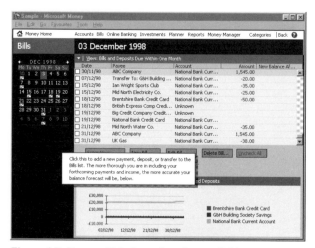

Figure 1.7: Pop-up Help for a function or field

The Money 98 Help file offers three types of help:

• Help Contents;

• Index; and

• Find.

Help Contents allows you to search for a Help Topic using general themes. Information is shown in greater detail by clicking on the icon representing a little book (see Figure 1.8). If you are used to printing Help topics, all you need to do is select the topic concerned and then click on the **Print** button at the bottom of the **Help Topics** window.

Figure 1.8: Access to the various Help topics from Help Contents

The Help Index allows you to search by keyword in the Money 98 Help file. This search function takes you directly to help associated with the keyword (see Figure 1.6). Keywords are listed in alphabetical order. It is recommended that you familiarise yourself with financial terminology in order to get the best out of this section of the index.

The final type of help is accessed by clicking on the **Find** tab. The first time this function is used, Money 98 offers to create an index of all words occurring in all Money 98 Help Topics. Follow the prompts given by the Find function (see Figure 1.9).

Figure 1.9: The Find function offers to index all words occurring in the text of all Help Topics. This indexing only takes place once

Any subsequent use of the Find function can then be carried out by keyword. It is only necessary to type the first few letters of the word you are searching for, and the Help program will offer the indexed keywords. When you select one of these keywords, you will then be offered the topic containing this word (see Figure 1.10). Simply click on a topic to consult it.

Figure 1.10: Word searching in Help Topics provides easy access

Hour 2

Creating and managing accounts

THE CONTENTS FOR THIS HOUR

- Creating a file
- Creating an account
- Deleting an account
- Closing an account
- The account register

CREATING A FILE

The first time you run Money 98, the Account Manager immediately offers to create a new file. This is the file in which all your accounts will be stored.

It is important to understand the difference between creating a new accounts file and creating a new account. You should not create an accounts file unless you want to separate different sets of accounts, such as home and business accounts. Accounts stored in different files cannot be combined for the compilation of reports. On the other hand, within a given file it is a simple matter to combine data from the various accounts contained within that file.

You can create as many files as you wish, subject to the limits of the disk space available on your system. Account reports and balances always refer to the accounts contained in the file currently being used.

Unless you are already familiar with accounting terminology and the use of Money 98, it is advisable to create two files. The first of these will be used for entering your actual, definitive accounting data, and the second for manipulating data while you are familiarising yourself with Money 98. This second file must not be given the same name as the working file. If you are managing your family accounts, for example, you might create a file named Family Accounts as the working file and another named Family Accounts Test as the test file.

 Create a new file only if you want to separate different sets of accounts, such as home and business accounts. It is not possible to generate reports or charts combining accounting elements from two different files.

If you already have proper accounting procedures – for example, if you are already using a previous version of Money or other accounting software – you can immediately create your account files and the accounts associated with these files:

1. Click on **File** on the menu bar to create a new file.

2. Next, click on **New**. The dialog box for creating a new file requests the name and type of file to be created.

3. Enter the name of the file in the **Name** field. The only type of file available is Microsoft Money, with the extension .mny (see Figure 2.1).

If a file is already in use, Money 98 offers to save this file before creating another.

CREATING AN ACCOUNT

Using the file opened by default when you start Money 98, you can create accounts to be managed in this file.

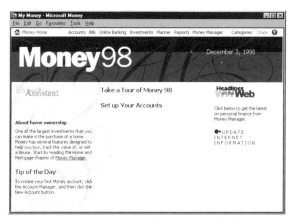

Figure 2.1: The appearance of the Money 98 Home screen when no account has been defined in the current file

1. Click on **Set Up Your Accounts** to create a new account. The **Account Manager** window appears.

2. At the bottom of the window, click on **New Account** (see Figure 2.2). This will start the New Account assistant.

3. Enter the name of the financial institution with which you hold the account to be managed (see Figure 2.3). If you have several accounts with one or more financial institutions, you will need to create that number of new accounts.

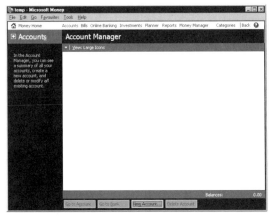

Figure 2.2: Account Manager window

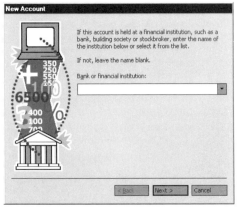

Figure 2.3: New Account assistant

Money 98 manages various types of account:

- **Asset.** Property: e.g. car, works of art, computer, etc. This information is useful when you need to calculate the net worth of your property, or when you make an insurance claim.

- **Other.** Items of income and expenditure which do not belong in any other type of account.

- **Bank.** Bank accounts other than current accounts or savings accounts and current account overdrafts.

- **Cash.** Cash income and spending, including money withdrawn from cash dispensers.

- **Visa Card.** For expenses paid by deferred-debit card.

- **Credit Card.** For expenses paid by credit cards other than Visa. Create a separate Money 98 account for each credit card.

- **Checking.** For keeping track of day-to-day expenses and bill payments.

- **Line of Credit.** For overdrafts arranged with a bank.

- **Savings.** Savings accounts held with financial institutions.

- **House.** Value of properties. This type of account is generally associated with a corresponding mortgage account.

- **Liability.** For managing money borrowed without interest, e.g. short-term loans or money borrowed from friends or family.

- **Investment.** For managing stocks and shares, bonds, open-end investment company holdings, etc.

- **Loan.** For managing money borrowed and repaid with interest in regular instalments (e.g. car loan, mortgage, consumer credit).

By default, the currency used for managing accounts in Money 98 is pounds sterling. When you create a new account you can, if you prefer, select a foreign currency and manage the account in this currency. In the event of any fluctuation in the value of this currency, you will need to adjust each transaction entered in this account according to the value of the currency on the date of entry. Transactions already entered on the basis of a different currency value will remain unchanged.

The procedure for creating an account is always the same:

1. Click on the **Accounts** button on the Navigation bar. The Account Manager shows the accounts being managed in the open file. If the file has just been created, it will not contain any accounts.

2. Click on **New Account** to begin creating an account. This button is situated in the lower right-hand part of the **Money 98** window.

3. The **New Account** window opens. Enter the name of the bank or other financial institution at which you hold an account. If you have already entered some accounts, you can choose from the list of existing institutions or leave the field blank.

4. Next, select the type of account from the list provided. Generally, if this is the first account to be created, the account type will be Current (see Figure 2.4).

Figure 2.4: Specifying the type of account to be created

5. After specifying the type of account, enter a name for this account. This is the name which will be displayed in the list of managed accounts.

6. Now specify the purpose of the account by selecting one of the following categories:

   – Spending Money;

   – Short-Term Savings;

   – Long-Term Savings; or

   – Other (see Figure 2.5).

For a current account, select the first option.

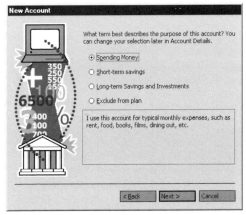

Figure 2.5: Specifying the type of account

7. Next, enter the account number. This number is not essential in order to use Money 98. If you do not have the account number to hand, you can enter it later under **Account Details**.

8. The next dialog box asks for the account balance and the working currency. Normally you will enter the ending balance from your last bank statement. If you want to include

Money 98

transactions which took place before the date on which the
account was created, enter the ending balance from an earlier
statement and then enter all transactions carried out since that
time. The working currency for this account is pounds sterling.
Select a different currency if required.

*With introduction of the euro, you will eventually find yourself
making mixed payments and deposits, i.e. in pounds and
euros. You will therefore need to create another account
with the same details but with the euro as the working
currency. Transactions conducted in pounds will be entered
in the managed account in pounds, while those conducted in
euros will be entered in euros. The procedures are explained
in detail in the chapter "From the pound to the euro".*

DELETING AN ACCOUNT

This is a quick and irreversible operation. If you delete an account,
all transactions contained in that account will also be permanently
deleted. Before deleting an account, you are strongly advised to
make a backup copy of your file.

While you are familiarising yourself with Money 98, the only time
you may need to delete an account is if you want to delete any
operations carried out for test purposes.

To delete an account:

1. Click on **Accounts** on the menu bar.

2. On the displayed list of accounts, click on the name of the
   account to be deleted.

3. Click on **Edit** on the menu bar.

4. Click on **Delete Account** (last line in the **Edit** window).

 22

5. Confirm the deletion of the account by clicking on **Yes** (see Figure 2.6).

Figure 2.6: Deleting an account is an irreversible operation

The selected account is permanently deleted. If you delete an account by accident, you can recover your file as follows:

1. Click on **File**.

2. Select **Restore Backup**.

3. Confirm restoration of the backup.

This recovery procedure is only possible if you have made a backup before deleting the account.

CLOSING AN ACCOUNT

You can close an account if it is no longer in use and you want to keep the recorded transactions:

1. Click on **Accounts** on the menu bar.

2. Click on the account to be closed in the main part of the window.

3. Click on **Edit** on the menu bar.

4. Click on **Account is Closed** (see Figure 2.7).

The name of this account now appears in the **Account Manager** window with an icon marked with a small red cross. The information in the account can still be consulted.

Figure 2.7: Close an account by selecting Edit and then Account is Closed

THE ACCOUNT REGISTER

The account register is where you enter all transactions for your various accounts:

- **Check** for all expenses paid by cheque;

- **Deposit** for all sums paid into your accounts;

- **Transfer** for all inter-account transfers;

- **Withdrawal** for all expenses paid by means other than cheque or bank card; and

- **Cash Machine** for all withdrawals of cash.

Each account has its own account register. It is important to enter all transactions in the appropriate account register for the corresponding account.

▬▬▬ Entering transactions

To enter a transaction, select an account and go into its account register:

1. Click on **Accounts** on the menu bar.

2. Select the account in which you want to enter transactions.

The account register is now displayed. If no transactions have yet been entered, the account register will be blank. Otherwise, the account register will display all transactions previously entered. Transactions already entered can be listed either partially or in full according to different sort methods, which are as follows:

- by date of entry;

- by order of entry;

- by number; or

- displaying unbalanced transactions only.

Transactions should be entered as regularly as possible. This will ensure that you can monitor your budget effectively. The accuracy of the accounting data depends on the care and regularity with which your accounting transactions are entered.

An expense paid by cheque would be entered as follows:

1. Click on **Check** (first tab in the account register).

2. Click on **New**.

3. In the appropriate boxes, enter the cheque number, the date on which it was issued and the amount.

4. Select the payee in the **Pay To** box. If the payee is not already entered in the list of available payees, create a new payee and select the relevant category and subcategory.

5. Enter any notes in the **Memo** box if required.

*Press the **Tab** key to move from one field to the next. You can get help on any field by pressing **F1** while the mouse cursor is positioned in that field.*

6. Confirm the entry by clicking on **Enter** (see Figure 2.8).

Figure 2.8: Entering and confirming a transaction in the account register

If you want to delete a transaction before it has been confirmed, click on **Cancel**.

Once transactions have been entered and confirmed, they are recorded automatically; they appear in the register above the transaction entry form.

Other transactions are entered in a similar manner to cheque payments:

- **Deposit.** All transactions representing income (e.g. salary, benefits, bonuses, gifts, refunds, etc.).

- **Transfer.** All transactions involving the transfer of money from one account to another, assuming you have more than one account (e.g. from a current account to a savings account).

- **Withdrawal.** All expenses paid by means other than cheque (e.g. direct debits, VISA payments, bank charges and administrative fees, etc.).

- **Cash Machine.** All withdrawals made in cash from a cash dispenser or automated telling machine at your bank.

If you do not want to manage the detail of your cash spending, enter any cash withdrawals in the account concerned with such withdrawals.

In order to know precisely how you are spending the money you withdraw in cash, create an account to manage this money. Define each withdrawal of cash from bank accounts as a transfer to the cash account. This transfer will appear as a credit in the cash account. Every day, make a note of each sum of cash spent and what it was used for. By entering each cash expense in the managed cash account, you will know the precise nature of your expenses.

Editing a transaction

It is not advisable to edit a recorded transaction. However, mistakes do happen, e.g. data errors, items entered under the wrong heading, items accidentally omitted, and so on.

To edit a transaction already entered:

1. Select the account to be amended.
2. Go into the account register for this account.
3. Locate the transaction concerned.
4. Select the transaction to be edited.
5. Click on **Edit** in the transaction entry zone.

You can edit the contents of any field for a given transaction. If you change items such as the date, number or amount, the account register will be updated automatically.

It is not possible to change the nature of a transaction, e.g. to change a Check transaction into a Withdrawal, other than by deleting the entry concerned and entering a new transaction.

Deleting a transaction

Transactions can be deleted once they have been entered in the
account register, but this is a somewhat risky operation:

1. Select the account to be amended.

2. Go into the account register for this account.

3. Locate the transaction concerned.

4. Select the transaction to be amended.

5. Click on **Edit** in the transaction entry zone.

6. Change the amount to zero, then click on **Enter**.

7. Click on **Delete the transaction** (see Figure 2.9).

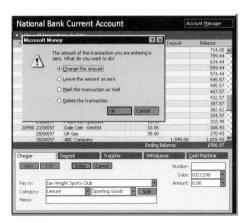

*Figure 2.9: Transactions can be deleted by entering a value of
zero in the Amount field*

Hour 3

Bills

The contents for this hour

- Scheduling bills
- Recording payments

In this hour, we will learn how to plan expenses and create forecast charts.

Scheduling bills

Throughout the year, you make payments which may be either recurring or one-off, but which are foreseeable. Similarly, you have income which is also foreseeable. All of these transactions will be entered in the Bill Calendar.

On the menu bar, click on Bills. Money 98 displays the Bill Calendar for all accounts contained in the open file (see Figure 3.1).

Figure 3.1: The Bill Calendar shows all expenses

▬▬▬ Entering a new transaction

This is the main function of the Bill Calendar. To enter a new transaction, select New Bill from the buttons offered by the Bill Calendar. This will open a dialog box which allows you to add a recurring payment (see Figure 3.2).

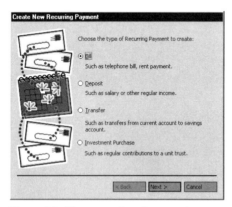

Figure 3.2: The procedure for entering a new transaction begins with this dialog box inviting you to specify the nature of the recurring payment

The various types of payment which can be entered in the Bill Calendar are as follows:

- debit transactions such as telephone bills and rent payments;

- credit transactions such as deposits of wages and family allowances;

- transfers, e.g. from a current account to a savings account; and

- investment purchases, e.g. regular contributions to a mutual fund.

Confirm the type of payment. For example, confirm that the payment concerned is a Bill, then click on Next at the bottom of the window (see Figure 3.2). Money 98 now displays an information window. Click on Next again to enter the transaction in the Bill Calendar.

Money 98 now opens a dialog box for entering a recurring transaction (see Figure 3.3):

1. Select the frequency of the transaction to be entered in the Bill Calendar. Various frequencies are available: daily, weekly, every other week, and so on up to every other year, and once-only transactions.

2. Select the entry method. By default, Manual Entry is selected. Other entry methods can be used for transactions carried out using Online Banking services.

3. Enter the details of the recurring transaction in the various fields.

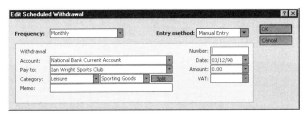

Figure 3.3: Dialog box for entering transactions involving recurring payments

Editing a transaction

The amounts for certain transactions can be amended. Any change in salary or benefits must be taken into account in the Bill Calendar. You can change the amount or any other parameter for these bills to update the Bill Calendar:

1. Click on the transaction to be amended.

2. Click on Edit Bill.

3. Edit one or more parameters for the transaction concerned.

Any amendments are automatically updated in the Bill Calendar.

To edit a particular instance of a transaction whose amount is not consistent, you will have to delete the entry for that instance and then make a new entry for a single payment.

Deleting a transaction

Transactions can easily be deleted from the Bill Calendar:

1. Select the transaction to be deleted.

2. Click on Delete Bill.

3. Click on one of the options offered in the Delete Recurring Payment window (see Figure 3.4).

Deletion of a recurring payment is an irreversible operation. If you delete such a payment by accident, you will have to enter it again. The deletion options are as follows:

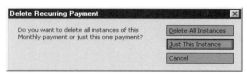

Figure 3.4: You can delete a single instance or all instances of a recurring payment

- **Delete All Instances.** All recurring payments for this bill are deleted. If you click on a future payment, all previous and subsequent payments will be deleted.

- **Just This Instance.** Only the selected instance is deleted. This option is useful for adjusting a payment which is foreseeable but for which a given instance is not consistent with other payment instances of the same type.

Monitoring due bills

Due bills can be monitored in two ways:

- every time you start Money 98; or

- every time you start your computer.

In the first case, start Money 98 and select Bills from the menu bar. On the left of the window is a small calendar. To change to view a different month, click on the left or right arrow on either side of the current month (see Figure 3.5).

Figure 3.5: The Bill Calendar allows you to select a particular month to view

On the calendar displayed for each month selected, small envelope icons are shown against days on which one or more bills are due for payment or collection. Click once on an envelope to display its corresponding payment.

When you start Windows, Money 98 reminds you of any due bills ten days in advance, and displays an icon in the Windows Taskbar to alert you to the fact that a bill entered in the Calendar is due.

To the left of each entry for due bills is a small box. If you double-click on an envelope displayed in the calendar, all bills due for payment up to that date will be shown with a check mark in this box. At the same time, in the column marked New Balance, the balance forecast is shown for each account covered by the Bill Calendar (see Figure 3.6).

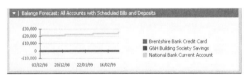

Figure 3.6: The Bill Calendar displays the balance forecast for each account

The balance forecast is calculated on the basis of the actual balance of each account and the transactions entered in the account register. If an account is in debit, the balance will be shown in red.

At the bottom of the Bill Calendar window you will see a graph showing the trend of the accounts covered by the Bill Calendar (see Figure 3.7). The horizontal axis indicates the dates for all due bills while the vertical axis indicates the balance forecast. This graph alerts you to the date of any critical situation affecting an account, and enables you to avoid crisis by taking the necessary precautions.

Figure 3.7: Graph showing account balance forecasts based on the transactions entered in the Bill Calendar

The Bill Calendar is a tool for planning your budget, but you can also enter exceptional items such as holidays, Christmas gifts, bonus payments, etc. by selecting a frequency of Only Once.

Even if the amounts of any exceptional expenses are only estimates, the Bill Calendar enables you to anticipate any crises. It would be absurd to find yourself in the position of managing your bills by means of a temporarily overdrawn account when another existing account could have covered this lack of funds. Long-term bill forecasts are rather unreliable, since the progress of your budget will depend on all expenses actually incurred.

RECORDING PAYMENTS

A due date has arrived, and the amount concerned has been paid or received. Record the payment in your account register as follows:

1. Click on Bills in the menu bar.

2. Check the box against the payment to be recorded (see Figure 3.8).

3. Click on Enter Now. This will open a dialog box.

4. Click on the Enter button on the right of the dialog box (see Figure 3.9).

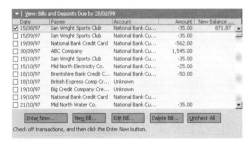

Figure 3.8: Select the payment to be recorded in the Bill Calendar

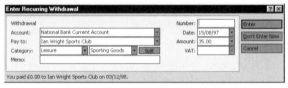

Figure 3.9: Details shown in the payment dialog box can be changed before the payment is recorded

If any of the details shown in the various fields of the dialog box are incomplete or incorrect, make any necessary corrections and then click on Enter.

The details entered in the dialog box are shown in the account register for the account associated with the payment concerned. Any payments you have recorded will no longer be displayed in the Bill Calendar.

 Payments due will be automatically deleted from the Bill Calendar if they are not recorded as paid. You are therefore strongly advised to record all payments.

If the amount of a payment is estimated, indicate this in the Memo field. You can go back into the account register to amend the entry and adjust it to match the actual payment. This situation might arise with payments which are made at regular intervals but whose amounts vary, such as telephone and electricity bills.

Hour 4

Advanced accounting operations

THE CONTENTS FOR THIS HOUR

- Splitting a transaction
- Balancing an account
- Working with foreign currencies

In this hour, we will look in detail at some advanced accounting operations, in particular, the splitting of certain items of income or expenditure, balancing accounts and the handling of foreign currencies.

SPLITTING A TRANSACTION

Certain transactions entered in account registers may relate to items of income or expenditure which fall into more than one category. For example, imagine that you have paid for some items purchased at a service station. Sometimes you might buy some snacks and some accessories for the maintenance of your car, but no fuel. In this example, the transaction cannot be entered under a single category, and it will be necessary to split the transaction.

▬▬▬ Entering a split transaction

Splitting a transaction allows you to assign different portions of a given expense to the relevant individual categories:

1. Select the account for which you need to enter a split transaction.

2. Click on the type of transaction to be entered (Check, Deposit, Transfer, etc.).

3. Complete the **Number**, **Date** and **Amount** fields.

4. Click on the **Split** button on the transaction form.

5. Enter one line for each separate element of the sum to be split (see Figure 4.1).

6. Click on **Done** to complete entry of the split transaction.

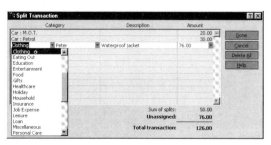

Figure 4.1: Entering the details of a split transaction

In the example given in Figure 4.1, you are splitting a transaction paid by cheque. Enter the total payment in the **Amount** field on the transaction form. Then, in the **Split Transaction** window, enter the details of the split amounts.

The **Split Transaction** window offers several columns:

- **Category.** Enter the details which you would normally have entered in the **Category** field on the transaction form.

- **Description.** Enter the details which you would normally have entered in the **Memo** field on the transaction form.

- **Amount.** Enter the amount corresponding to the split transaction.

*You can move between fields by clicking directly on the field in which you want to enter details, or by using the **Tab** key to move from one field to the next.*

While you are entering details for the split transaction, two lines at the bottom of the **Split Transaction** window show the amount which has not yet been assigned, and the total amount of the transaction.

The amount not yet assigned corresponds to the difference between the total for the details already entered for the split transaction and the total amount of the transaction as a whole. This amount should be zero when all the separate elements of the transaction have been recorded. The total amount of the transaction corresponds to the value entered in the **Amount** field on the transaction form.

If you confirm the details of a split transaction when the total of the split elements does not match the total amount of the transaction as a whole, a warning box appears with suggestions for possible solutions (see Figure 4.2):

- Edit the split amounts.

- Change the total transaction amount. Selecting this option will amend the **Amount** field on the transaction form.

- Reallocate the unassigned amount. If you choose this option, enter the details for the corresponding transactions.

- Continue without assigning the amount concerned.

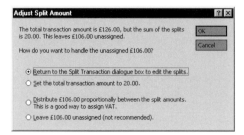

Figure 4.2: Window for adjusting split amounts

If you select the last option when a split transaction has an unassigned amount, this will not change the total transaction amount. The unassigned amount will not appear in the details shown for accounts allocated to a category.

You are strongly advised not to use the last option: the total amount of a split transaction should always correspond to the sum of the split elements.

Editing a split transaction

Once a split transaction has been confirmed, the details shown for transactions associated with the account will not give any indication of a split transaction other than the date and amount of the transaction concerned. You can check the details of the transaction and edit them if required:

1. Select the split transaction you want to view or edit.

2. Right-click while the cursor is positioned over the transaction selected above. A drop-down menu appears.

3. Click on **Split**. The **Split Transaction** window appears (see Figure 4.3).

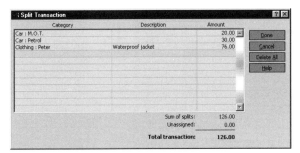

Figure 4.3: Displaying details of a split transaction

4. Edit the details of the split transaction as required.

When you select a split transaction, the word "Split" will be displayed on the transaction form.

After selecting a split transaction, you can also view the transaction details by clicking on the **Edit** button and then the **Split** button on the transaction form (see Figure 4.3).

BALANCING AN ACCOUNT

Balancing your accounts enables you to check the details shown on your bank statements. You should balance your accounts whenever you receive a new statement from your financial institution. This operation will enable you to detect any errors made by your bank – or by you – in the handling of your accounts.

1. Have your most recent statement to hand.

2. Select the account to be balanced. On the lower left of the **Account Manager** window, click on **Balance**.

3. A window appears, offering to adjust the account balance, or balance the account. To balance the account, click on **Balance** (see Figure 4.4).

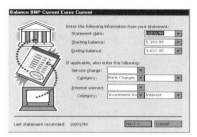

Figure 4.4: Account Balance window

4. In the **Starting Balance** and **Ending Balance** fields, enter the starting and ending balances shown on your statement.

5. If applicable, enter any service charges paid and interest earned during the period covered by this statement. Then click on **Next**.

6. Note the information displayed on the left of the screen, and then clear each of the transactions shown on your statement by clicking in the **C** field of the Account Register (see Figure 4.5).

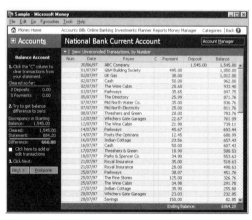

Figure 4.5: Balance the account by clearing each transaction in the account register

All bank statements for a given year are numbered incrementally in the order of their issue. In the event of any lack of continuity in the numbering of statements, you should request a duplicate of the missing statement or statements. These are important accounting documents which must be retained and presented in the event of a tax inspection or any dispute with your financial institution.

7. Once you have cleared all items of income and expenditure shown on your statement, click on **Next** and follow the instructions shown on screen.

The reconciliation procedure is now complete. All reconciled transactions are indicated by the letter **R** (Reconciled) in column C (Cleared).

If it has not been possible to balance the account with the contents of your bank statements, Money 98 informs you that there is an

- **Go back to balancing the account.** This option returns you to the previous stage and allows you to insert any transactions you may have omitted during a previous session.

- **Use AutoReconcile.** This option adjusts the account according to the balance shown on the statement by means of an adjustment operation which will be recorded under the heading Account Adjustment.

- **Automatically adjust the account balance.** This is similar to the preceding option, with the difference that Money 98 asks for a category for the account adjustment. If you do not select a category, Money 98 creates an adjustment operation in the account register.

When balancing an account, it is essential to work with your most recent statement. All previous statements should already have been balanced. If this is not the case, balance earlier statements first.

At the end of a account balancing procedure, the balance of transactions entered up until the date of the statement should match the balance shown on the statement at that date. If this is not the case, there are several possible explanations:

- There has been an error in an account entry or in the compilation of a bank statement.

- A payment has not been cashed by the payee. If this is the case, the payment will appear on a later statement and the accounts will be rebalanced.

- A transaction has not been cleared, or has been cleared by mistake in place of another transaction.

In all these cases, Money 98 allows account entries to be corrected, added or deleted: account balancing is designed to detect these errors.

If a transaction has been mistakenly marked as reconciled, select the transaction concerned and right-click. Select **Mark As**, followed by **Unreconciled** (see Figure 4.6).

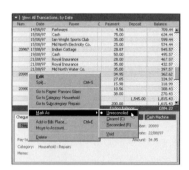

Figure 4.6: A transaction marked as reconciled can be reclassed as unreconciled

If you change any transactions which have formed the subject of an account-balancing procedure, it is advisable to delete any Adjustment shown in the account register and then balance the account again.

WORKING WITH FOREIGN CURRENCIES

The euro was introduced in January 1999, and will start appearing in our change in 2002. The transition from the pound to the euro is explained in detail in Hour 12. Even now, however, many users of Money 98 find themselves dealing with payments in foreign currencies.

Money 98 is perfectly capable of handling transactions conducted in foreign currencies.

Creating an account in a foreign currency

To create an account in a foreign currency, proceed as you would to create an account in pounds sterling. During the procedure for creating a new account, select the working currency for this account. If no exchange rate is defined, Money 98 will ask you to specify a rate for the currency concerned. This will be the applicable exchange rate for changing the selected currency into the working currency of the file, currently pounds sterling.

Once the foreign currency account has been created, it can be consulted in the same way as any other existing account in the current file. Check the parameters for the foreign currency account by selecting the account created and then clicking on **Details** (see Figure 4.7).

Figure 4.7: In the account created here, the currency used is Swiss francs

Transactions in foreign currencies are recorded in exactly the same way as other account entries. The only difference is that the transaction amounts are in a foreign currency. Money 98 will automatically convert the account balance into pounds when compiling any reports or creating payee accounts.

The global balance for all accounts is shown in pounds (see Figure 4.8).

Num	Date	Payee	C	Payment	Deposit	Balance
3265	18/12/98			91.30		87,694.70
3266	18/12/98	St. Andrews Hospital		322.24		87,372.46

View: All Transactions, by Date

Ending Balance: £87,372.46

Figure 4.8: The global balance of accounts combines all individual account balances, including those for any foreign currency accounts

▰▰▰ Entering a transaction in a foreign currency

Entering a transaction conducted in a foreign currency into an account managed in pounds is similar to entering a transaction conducted in pounds:

1. Open an existing account.

2. Click on the type of transaction to be recorded (Check, Deposit, Transfer, etc.).

3. When you are ready to enter the amount, press **F8**.

4. Enter the relevant details in the **Currency Converter** window (see Figure 4.9).

The transaction will be incorporated in the account register, with the amount entered in foreign currency being converted into pounds.

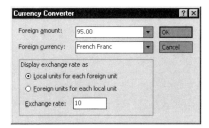

Figure 4.9: Entering the amount in a foreign currency in the
Currency Converter window

Check that the foreign currency amount converted into
pounds and the figure shown on your bank statement are
consistent. If necessary, adjust this figure when you balance
the account.

More detailed operations involving entries in foreign currencies
are explained in Hour 12.

Hour 5

Categories and classifications

THE CONTENTS FOR THIS HOUR

- Predefined categories
- Working with categories and subcategories
- Classifications
- Payees

When you enter a transaction in an account register, you specify a category for this transaction. These categories enable you to determine the nature of all items of income and expenditure. With the help of Money 98, you can easily review the totals associated with each category.

At the end of the year, you will be able to see what proportion of your overall budget has been spent on each category by retrieving the details of your spending in each category.

PREDEFINED CATEGORIES

Money 98 includes a number of categories and subcategories. You can easily consult these by clicking on **Categories** on the menu bar. The list of categories will then be displayed (see Figure 5.1).

Figure 5.1: The list of categories allows you to review the transactions associated with each category and subcategory

On the left-hand side of the window containing the list of categories, you can select from the following options:

- **Payees**. This is the list of all parties with whom you have conducted financial transactions (clients, creditors, debtors, etc.);

- **Categories**. This is the list displayed by default when you select **Categories** from the menu bar; and

- **Classifications 1 and 2.** These two options allow you to display any customised categories.

The list of categories is divided into two types:

- income; and

- expenses.

Under each of these headings, you will find predefined categories and associated subcategories. When you enter a transaction in an account register, you assign it to a category and a subcategory. By using the Categories list, you can easily review all transactions falling within a given category or subcategory.

When you enter a transaction in an account register, only the name of the category allows you to determine whether the transaction concerned represents income or expenditure. In the event of any mistake, Money 98 displays a warning message.

To view details for a given category, select with the mouse the category concerned and double-click on it. The accounting and tax information for this category will then be displayed (see Figure 5.2).

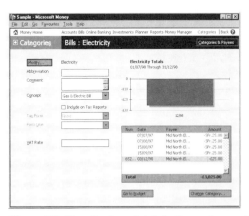

Figure 5.2: The display of details for a given category gives you access to the transactions assigned to that category

The display of details for a given category gives you access to various information:

- on the left of the screen, immediately beneath the menu bar, is the category selector. On the right is the name of the category currently being displayed;

- the left-hand side of the remainder of the screen shows the parameters for the current category; and

- the right-hand side shows the accounting data for the current category.

A chart is displayed in the upper right-hand part of the screen. This chart shows trends in income or expenses for the current category. The table in the lower part of the screen shows all accounting data entered and assigned to this category. The total displayed beneath this table represents the sum of all income or expenditure for this category since the beginning of the year.

WORKING WITH CATEGORIES AND SUBCATEGORIES

The categories and subcategories offered by Money 98 may not be enough to reflect the individual circumstances of your accounting and tax situation. You can create new categories and subcategories which can then be renamed, moved or deleted.

▄▄▄ Creating categories and subcategories

You can create a new category or subcategory when entering a transaction as follows:

1. Click on **Accounts** and select an account.

2. Click on one of the options for entering a transaction (**Check**, **Deposit**, **Transfer**, etc.).

3. Enter the transaction.

4. In the **Category** field, enter a name for a new category not listed by Money 98. This will open a dialog box for defining a new category (see Figure 5.3).

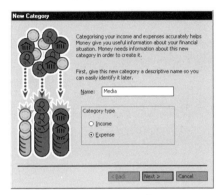

Figure 5.3: Creating a new Expense category named Media

5. Confirm the category name by clicking on **Next**. In the following window, select one of the predefined category groups (see Figure 5.4). Confirm your selection by clicking on **Finish**.

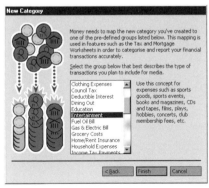

Figure 5.4: Assigning the Expense category named Media to the Entertainment group

6. Now, on the transaction form, go to the field immediately to the right of the name of the category just created. Specify a subcategory to be associated with the new category. Money 98 will open a window asking you to confirm that this subcategory should be associated with the category indicated (see Figure 5.5).

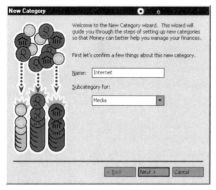

Figure 5.5: Creating an Internet subcategory associated with the Media category

7. Confirm the creation of the subcategory by clicking on **Next**.

8. Select the group associated with the subcategory you have just created (see Figure 5.4).

You can also create new categories or subcategories via the **Categories** option on the menu bar:

• **Creating a new category.** The options for this are identical to those offered when you create a new category on the transaction form (see Figures 5.3 and 5.5).

• **Creating a new subcategory.** The options for this are identical to those offered when you create a new subcategory on the transaction form (see Figures 5.4 and 5.5).

Renaming categories and subcategories

Categories and subcategories can only be renamed by using the Categories function on the menu bar:

1. Click on **Categories** on the menu bar.

2. Select the category or subcategory to be renamed.

3. Click on **Modify**.

4. Enter a new name for the category or subcategory concerned (see Figure 5.6).

All accounts associated with the old name for the modified category or subcategory will use the new name. Take care to give your categories and subcategories names which will be easily remembered.

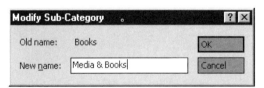

Figure 5.6: Renaming a subcategory

Do not give a subcategory a name already used by an existing category.

Deleting categories and subcategories

You can delete a category or subcategory at any time:

1. Click on **Categories** on the menu bar.

2. Select the category or subcategory to be deleted.

3. Click on **Delete** in the lower right-hand part of the active window.

If transactions have been assigned to the category or subcategory concerned, Money 98 will display a warning and offer to reassign these transactions to another category. If you do not reassign these transactions, they will have no category (see Figure 5.7).

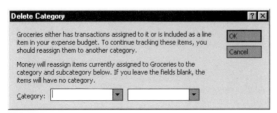

Figure 5.7: Reassigning the transactions associated with a category to be deleted

 Transactions which are not assigned to a category will be incorporated in your overall account balance, but will not be shown in reports.

CLASSIFICATIONS

Classifications are mainly designed for Money 98 users who want to manage certain specific aspects of their budget independently of the general categories. For example, if you own rented properties or manage various projects, classifications will help you to organise your transactions in a different way.

By using classifications, you can group your transactions:

- by client or project;
- by property or lot; or
- by professional or personal expenses.

You can create a maximum of two classifications, each of which may contain classes and subclasses. Classifications are ordered and managed in a similar way to categories and subcategories.

Creating a classification

For example, let us consider the management of rented properties.
You own some rented properties and want to create a Properties
classification, along with associated classes and subclasses:

1. Click on **Categories** on the menu bar.

2. Click on **Classification 1** on the left-hand side of the
   Categories window.

3. The **Add Classification** dialog box appears. Select one of the
   predefined classifications. For the purposes of this example,
   choose the **Properties** classification.

4. Confirm the new classification by clicking on **OK** (see Figure 5.8).

Creating classes for a classification

Creating classes and subclasses for a classification is similar to
creating categories and subcategories:

1. Select the classification you have created – **Properties**, in our
   example. If no classes have yet been created, the list of classes
   will be empty.

Figure 5.8: The Add Classification dialog box

2. Click on **New**. Enter a name for the class you want to create,
   then click on **OK**.

3. To create a subclass within the class you have created, select the class concerned and then click on **New** once again.

4. Money 98 offers to create a new class or subclass within the selected class. Choose **New Subclass** and enter a name for this subclass.

The list of classes and subclasses will show all items you have entered (see Figure 5.9). In our example, two properties and two apartments per property have been created.

Once you have created a classification, Money 98 adds an extra field to the transaction form, beneath the **Category** and **Subcategory** fields (see Figure 5.10).

Figure 5.9: List of classes and subclasses created within the Properties classification

Figure 5.10: Two extra classification fields

Using classifications

A classification represents a particular aspect of your life which needs to be identified and managed separately. By defining a classification, you will be able to keep track of a subset of your transactions. Classifications are used when you enter your transactions:

1. Select **Accounts** and then an individual account. When entering a transaction, select the **Classification** field located beneath the **Category** field. This field is marked with the name you assigned to the classification created.

2. Select the relevant class from the list.

3. If applicable, select a subclass from the list.

4. Complete the other fields, including the **Category** and **Subcategory** fields (see Figure 5.10).

Deleting a classification or class

Deleting a classification has no effect on transactions grouped together by categories. Only the fields corresponding to the classification concerned will be removed.

1. Select **Categories** on the menu bar. Select a classification.

2. Click on the **Delete** button in the lower left-hand part of the screen.

To delete a class or subclass, select it and then click on **Delete** at the bottom of the screen.

 Deleting a class within a classification will also delete all subclasses associated with that class.

PAYEES

Payees are individuals or institutions to whom you make payments or from whom you receive payments.

Payees are created automatically when you enter transactions in an account register. With Money 98, it is very easy to group together all income or expenses associated with a particular payee.

Creating a payee

In addition to the automatic creation of a payee via the transaction form, you can also create payees by using the **Categories** function on the menu bar:

1. Click on **Categories** on the menu bar.

2. Click on **Payees** on the left-hand side of the screen.

3. Click on **New** at the bottom of the screen.

4. Enter the details of the new payee, then confirm by clicking on **OK** (see Figure 5.11).

Figure 5.11: Entering the name of a new payee

Payee names correspond to the names of the clients, suppliers and companies with which you conduct financial transactions.

Displaying payee details

This function enables you to consult information about a given payee and all transactions associated with that payee:

1. On the menu bar, click on Categories.

2. Click on Payees.

3. Select a payee from the list.

4. Click on Categories and Payee at the top of the screen (see Figure 5.12).

You can also display payee details by double-clicking on the name of a payee.

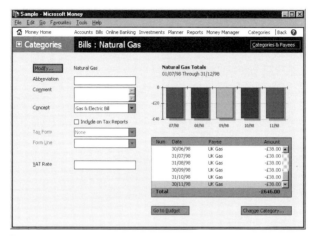

Figure 5.12: Displaying details about a payee

The window displays all information about the selected payee. If you wish, you can enter additional details for the payee concerned (e.g. address). In our example, we have selected a payee named Petrol. If you had bought fuel from more than one service station, you would leave the information fields blank.

The chart in the upper right-hand part of the window indicates the volume of transactions conducted with this payee. The table in the lower right-hand part of the window gives an itemised summary of all transactions conducted with this payee.

Changing the name or details of a payee has no effect on the transactions entered in relation to that payee.

Deleting a payee has no effect on the categories and subcategories associated with transactions conducted with that payee.

The transactions associated with a payee can be classed under different categories. For example, purchases made in a department store might be entered in categories such as Food, Clothing, Car, etc.

Exploring transactions associated with a given payee

The chart displayed in the payee information window gives you access to all transactions conducted with the payee concerned.

Position the mouse cursor over one of the bars in the chart and click once. A small box will appear showing the total transactions conducted with the payee concerned during the month selected. For example, if you position the cursor over the bar corresponding to the month of August, the box will show the total of all transactions conducted with this payee during the month of August (see Figure 5.13).

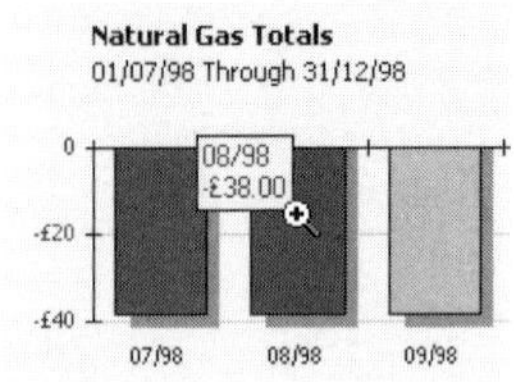

Figure 5.13: Displaying the monthly total of transactions conducted with a given payee

If you double-click on one of the bars in the chart, you will be taken to a window showing an itemised summary of all transactions conducted with the payee concerned during the month selected (see Figure 5.14).

You can create a report by clicking on the button marked **Create a Report**. We will deal with reports in greater detail in the next hour.

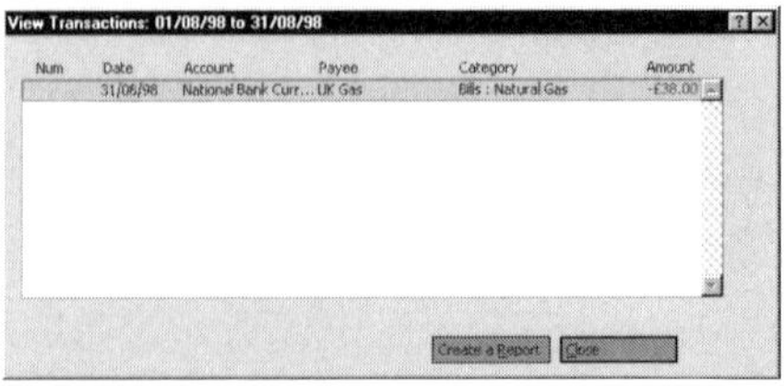

Figure 5.14: Itemised summary of transactions conducted with a given payee during the month selected

Hour 6

Reports and charts

THE CONTENTS FOR THIS HOUR

- Accounting reports and charts
- Customising reports
- Copying and exporting reports or charts
- Printing reports

In this hour, we will explore the most interesting aspect of Money 98: its wide range of reports, including graphical reports, which are the real strength of the program.

ACCOUNTING REPORTS AND CHARTS

Reports and charts give you a visual representation of the state and trends of your finances. These reports and charts can be printed or exported to other documents. Money 98 offers 29 different types of reports and charts, divided into six categories:

- Spending Habits;

- What I Have;

- What I Owe;

- Investments;

- Taxes; and

- Monthly Reports (only in Money Financial Suite).

In all these types, you can display precisely the information required. You can create a **Favorites** list, in which you can enter an unlimited number of reports and charts. This will give you very quick access to the reports you use most frequently, including any customised reports.

 *There is no limit to the number of reports which can be entered in the **Favorites** list. Money records the customisation applied to a report, not the actual information shown in the report. Every time you consult a report, Money will retrieve its up-to-date details.*

Displaying a report or chart

Reports and charts are accessible from the menu bar, but certain charts are also available via other functions of Money 98:

1. On the menu bar, click on **Reports**.

2. Select the type of report or chart desired by clicking on one of the categories listed on the left-hand part of the screen.

3. Click once on the name of the report or chart required. At the bottom of the screen, you will see a brief description of the type of information displayed by the report or chart concerned (see Figure 6.1).

4. Click on **Go to Report/Chart** at the bottom of the screen to display the chart selected (see Figure 6.2).

Figure 6.1: Selecting a chart

To change the bar chart to a line chart or pie chart, click on one of the icons shown at the bottom of the screen.

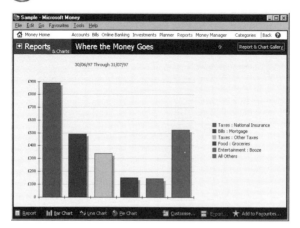

Figure 6.2: Display of the selected chart

When you position the mouse cursor over a bar or sector in a chart, one of two symbols will appear:

- If a small lens with a plus (+) sign is shown, this means you can display details by double-clicking on the chart or on the line of the report. This will take you to details of the transactions associated with the displayed chart.

- If a small lens with no sign is shown, only the exact amount corresponding to the chart concerned will be displayed in a small box to one side of the lens.

If you would like quicker access to the chart or report concerned, click on **Add to Favorites**. The next time you click on **Reports**, you will be taken to the **Favorites** list, from which you can retrieve the chart or report with your chosen appearance and parameters.

CUSTOMISING REPORTS

The appearance and content of reports and charts can be modified so that they show what you want to see. To do this:

1. Select a report or chart.

2. Click on **Customize**.

3. In the **Customize Chart** window, make any changes by selecting from the available options. To change the style and size of the characters used, click on **Fonts** (see Figure 6.3).

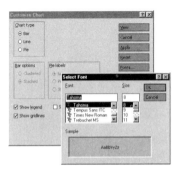

Figure 6.3: Customize Chart window and Select Font window

4. Confirm your customisation by clicking on **View**.

5. Click on **Add to Favorites** to record this definitive configuration.

Chart customisation options are as follows:

- **Chart type:** bar chart, line chart or pie chart;

- **Clustered or stacked bars:** this option cannot be used with all chart types; and

- **Pie labels:** none, percentages or amounts in pounds.

Two further selections, **Fonts** and **Options**, are available via the buttons in the right-hand part of the **Customize Chart** window:

- **Fonts button:** this allows you to change the size, style and font of characters used in the selected report or chart; and

- **Options button:** this takes you to the **Customize Report** window (see Figure 6.4). For example, the **Dates** field is very useful for specifying the period to be taken into account for data displayed in the report or chart concerned.

If you add the chart or report to the **Favorites** list, it will be more readily accessible and will take account of your customised parameters.

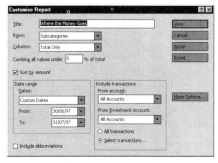

Figure 6.4: Customize Report window

*When customising a report or chart, you can preview its appearance by clicking on **Apply**.*

COPYING AND EXPORTING REPORTS OR CHARTS

The usefulness of a financial management tool is not confined to its accounting functions, even when the tool is as powerful as Money 98. It may also be useful to be able to retrieve the data displayed in reports or charts and incorporate it in other documents such as reports and correspondence.

Copying and pasting via the Clipboard

The simplest way of retrieving data is to use the Windows Clipboard function. Data is transferred from one application to another via the Clipboard as follows:

1. Select and display a report or chart.

2. On the function bar at the top of the screen, click on **Edit** and then **Copy**. The chart or report will be copied into the Windows clipboard.

3. Open another Windows application, e.g. WordPad or Microsoft Word.

4. Click on **Edit** again, then **Paste**. The report or chart will be incorporated into the current document (see Figure 6.5).

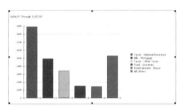

Figure 6.5: Example of a chart copied and pasted into a Word document via the Clipboard

Exporting a report

To incorporate data from a report into a spreadsheet program, you must use the Export function, which generates an intermediate document compatible with the Import function of the spreadsheet program. The same procedure is followed to retrieve data into a word-processor or other program capable of importing a report:

1. Select a report.

2. Click on **Export**.

3. Enter a name for the exported file. The file containing the exported data will be in plain text format. Each line contains a single line of the report, with the columns separated by a Tab character.

4. Retrieve the exported file into the application of your choice, e.g. word-processor, spreadsheet program.

PRINTING REPORTS

Money 98 reports and charts can be printed on any monochrome or colour printer. The quality of reproduction depends on the type and performance of the printer used. Before you print, check the printing parameters:

1. Click on **File** on the menu bar.

2. Click on **Print Setup**.

3. Select a destination printer if the printer shown by default is not the one you want to use (see Figure 6.6).

4. Make any necessary changes to the printing set-up.

Figure 6.6: Selecting a destination printer and setting the printing options

If the printer you want to use does not appear in the displayed list, you will need to install it from Windows. Consult Windows documentation for information on how to do this.

Changing printing parameters in Money 98 will not affect print options for other Windows applications.

Once you have set the printing parameters, you are ready to print the report or chart concerned:

1. Select the report or chart to be printed.

2. On the menu bar, click on **Print**.

 On a monochrome printer, colours will be translated into shades of grey. Any characters or graphical elements which are pale may be difficult or even impossible to read.

Hour 7

Portfolio management

THE CONTENTS FOR THIS HOUR

- Introducing the Portfolio
- Investment transactions
- Updating prices

While most people with modest savings put their surplus funds in savings accounts offering a fixed but low rate of return, others invest on the stock market. The risks are greater, but those who are fortunate enough to invest well can reap substantial rewards.

The Investments function of Money 98 will be of great help in managing and tracking such investments, whether this is done daily or periodically. Moreover, the features providing access to online services, in particular via the Internet, will allow you to monitor your portfolio of stocks and shares quickly and efficiently.

INTRODUCING THE PORTFOLIO

Managing shares or bonds requires the use of functions which are not available for the management of bank, savings or credit card accounts. All shares are grouped together in a portfolio, which we will now learn to create and manage.

Click on **Investments** on the menu bar. You will see a list of all securities held, along with their prices. You can carry out any operation you choose on these items. You can:

- add or modify investment transactions;
- view trends in the performance of investments;
- check the distribution of securities and display investment details in various ways; and
- update investment prices, either manually or electronically.

Investments include mutual funds, shares, bonds and retirement pension funds.

 A mutual fund is a body of funds constituted by multiple investors. When you subscribe to a mutual fund, e.g. open-end investment company or common investment fund, your money is invested along with that of other investors.

Investment accounts contain groups of investments whose values are variable. Generally, the transactions associated with these investment accounts are taken care of by financial institutions or brokers.

Investments are entered into these investment accounts, and a given investment account may contain several investments. Similarly, several different types of investment may be handled by your broker or financial institution.

Investment accounts are used for:

- **Shares:** premium options, Treasury bills and Treasury bonds;

- **Bonds:** savings bonds, etc; and

- **Deposit certificates:** mutual funds.

For a retirement pension scheme, you would set up a retirement pension account.

Once you have entered your investment transactions, you will be able to review their price trends, check the portfolio value, show investments which have either risen or fallen in price, and pass on any gains or deficits to your tax return.

Creating investment accounts

This is the first step before entering your investments. You must create a separate investment account for each type of statement you receive. You can enter investments as soon as you have created these investment accounts. To create your investment accounts, have all your investment documentation to hand and then proceed as follows:

1. On the Money 98 menu bar, click on **Investments**.

2. Click on **New** (second button from the right at the bottom of the screen).

3. Select **A new Investment Account** (see Figure 7.1).

4. Click on **Next**, then follow the instructions shown.

5. Enter a name for the investment account. Generally, this will take the form of <bank name> Investment (e.g. BRED Investment). Click on **Next**.

6. Answer **Yes** or **No** when asked whether the investments in the account concerned are tax-deferred. If they are not tax-deferred, then any gains will appear on your tax reports. Click on **Next**.

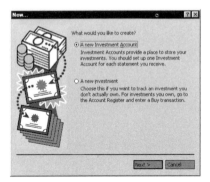

Figure 7.1: Creating an investment account

7. Enter the estimated value of the investments to be assigned to this investment account, and specify whether the account has an associated cash account for any money which is not reinvested. Click on **Next**.

8. Enter the ending balance shown on the last statement, or a value of zero if you want to start monitoring the value of the investments from the day you open the investment account. Specify the working currency for the account. By default, Money 98 proposes the currency associated with the investment management body, normally pounds sterling. Click on **Next**.

9. Specify the purpose of the account: Spending Money, Short-Term Savings, etc. Click on **Next**.

The inset box beneath the buttons for specifying the purpose of the account provides a detailed explanation of the meaning of each button.

Create a separate investment account for each statement, even if you receive several statements from the same financial institution. This will make it easier to retrieve the transactions associated with each respective statement.

Creating investments

Now you have created your investment account, it is time to add your investments:

1. On the menu bar, click on **Investments**.

2. Select the investment account in which you want to enter the new investment.

3. Click on **New** (second button from the right at the bottom of the screen).

4. Select **A new Investment** and click on **Next**.

5. Enter a name for the investment and specify the type of investment, then click on **Next**.

6. Enter the stock symbol (quotation code), the status of the investment (i.e. whether it is tax exempt) and any comments. Click on **Finish**.

This new investment will appear in the portfolio as soon as you have conducted any transactions (buying or selling) in relation to the investment.

INVESTMENT TRANSACTIONS

Now that you have created your investment accounts and the investments associated with them, you can conduct buying and selling transactions in relation to these investments. You can enter investment values at any time, and these will be taken into account in calculating the global value of your investment portfolio. Entering investment values on a regular basis will enable you to monitor trends in the value of your portfolio.

Entering investment transactions

Investment transactions involve the buying and selling of securities. All buying transactions are debited against the spending account associated with the investment account; conversely, all selling transactions are credited to that account.

1. Click on **Accounts** on the menu bar.

2. Open the investment account in which you want to enter transactions.

3. Click on the **New** button above the transaction form. The first data entry fields will appear.

4. In the **Investment** field, select the investment for which you want to enter the transaction concerned (see Figure 7.2).

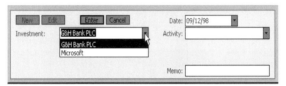

Figure 7.2: Selecting an investment

5. Select the type of activity concerned (see Figure 7.3).

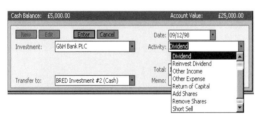

Figure 7.3: Selecting an activity

6. Complete the other fields, in particular the **Quantity**, **Price** and **Commission** fields.

7. Confirm the transaction by clicking on **Enter**.

 *If, in the **Investment** field, you specify an investment other than those listed, Money 98 will open the Create New Investment assistant and create the investment for you.*

If you buy a given investment in multiple lots, you must enter a separate transaction for each purchase. For example, if you buy 50 FT shares in January and then another 50 in March, you must enter two Buy transactions.

Do not forget to fill in the **Commission** and **Transfer From** fields.

- The **Commission** field corresponds to the commission charged by the institution issuing the buying or selling orders. The **Total** field will be automatically updated to show the overall total for the share purchase and the commission. Consequently, you do not need to enter anything in this field.

- The **Transfer From** field indicates the spending account to or from which you are crediting or debiting the transaction. This is not necessarily the spending account with the financial institution issuing the buying or selling orders.

- The **Memo** field allows you to enter a comment on this purchase.

The balance for the investment account should be updated whenever you receive new statements from your financial institution.

UPDATING PRICES

The buying and selling of investments is something of a lottery. You might choose to have blind faith in the securities you are dealing with, and take no notice of the prices notified to you when you receive your account statement. The prices shown on this statement are the ones that must be entered in Money 98.

Updating prices manually

The procedure for updating prices manually is not complicated, but it is repetitive:

1. On the menu bar, click on **Investments**.

2. Select the investment you want to update.

3. Click on **Update Price** (lower left of the screen).

4. Select the date and enter the price corresponding to this date (see Figure 7.4).

Figure 7.4: Updating a share price

5. Click on **Update**.

The balance of accounts shows the combined total for all accounts, including investment accounts. A spending account may be overdrawn even though the global balance is in credit.

Updating investment prices is of value only for the date corresponding to a given fixed price. To determine the precise value of a portfolio, you must update the prices of all your investments to show their values on the date of purchase. Quotation values can be obtained from your financial broker or via stock-market information services available on the Internet. If you monitor your investment portfolio every day, we strongly recommend that you use the Internet if you are not already doing so. Refer to Appendix 1, which gives links to various servers providing financial and legal information and news.

Keeping a regular record of the prices of your investments will enable you to monitor the fluctuations of each investment. At any time, you can enter all prices quoted between any two given dates.

To do this, go to the **Update Price** window for the investment concerned, click on the arrow at the right of the **Date** field, and then select the date by clicking on the calendar the date of the investment update (see Figure 7.5).

Figure 7.5: Selecting the date in the calendar

 You can change the month for the date selection by clicking on the two left- and right-pointing arrows on either side of the month name displayed at the top of the calendar.

Money 98 updates the investment account balance using the most recently entered value at the time of the portfolio update.

Some financial institutions offer their clients automatic price updates. If you are interested in this service, be sure to ask the broker managing your investments about availability and access conditions for this type of service.

Updating prices automatically

At the risk of labouring the point, it is advisable to have access to the Internet. If you do not yet have such access, you can obtain this from various service providers. If you already have Internet access, proceed as follows to automatically update the prices of your investments:

1. Click on **Investments** on the menu bar.

2. Click on **Online Quotes** at the bottom of the screen.

3. In the **Online Services** window, select the prices for which you want an automatic online update (see Figure 7.6).

Figure 7.6: Selecting prices for online updating

4. Click on **Call**, and the connection will be established. The **Connecting** window shows the progress of the investment update (see Figure 7.7).

Figure 7.7: Display of the progress of an automatic price update

*If this is your first connection to the Internet using Money 98, you should first click on **Settings** to tell Money how you want to connect to the Internet.*

Once the update has completed, you can check that the prices of your investments have been included in this automatic update. Proceed as though you were carrying out a manual update: in the **Update Price** window, you should find the prices previously entered and the most recent price downloaded automatically.

The automatically updated price is labelled Online. This price represents the official stock-market quotation, subject to a time-lag of between one and 30 minutes behind the real-time quotation price.

Share prices fluctuate within the space of a single day. The price downloaded automatically is only an isolated snapshot from the range of prices which may apply to the share concerned during the course of that day.

Automatic updates are particularly useful when you want to monitor an investment portfolio on a daily basis. Prices downloaded by Money 98 are immediately incorporated in the relevant investment accounts, enabling you to check your account balances immediately.

Money 98 needs the code for a given investment before it can download the corresponding price. This code is shown on your account statement. Alternatively, it can easily be found on stock-market information sites (see Appendix 1).

▄▄▄▄ Access to subscription quotes

If you have a modem but no Internet access, you can update the prices of your investments by using the Subscription Quotes service. This service is subject to monthly subscription charges. To use this service:

1. Click on **Investments** on the menu bar.

2. Click on **Online Quotes**, then **Settings**.

3. Click on **Subscription Quotes**, then **Next**.

4. Click on **Open Application Form**. Print the form, then complete and return it.

You will be contacted by the supplier of subscription quotes, who will tell you when you will receive quotes, as well as inform you about the applicable regulations and how to use your modem.

The quotes supplied by this service are subject to a time-lag of 30 minutes behind the real-time quotation.

Checking investment transactions

Check the consistency of your investment transactions with the statements relating to your investment account:

1. Have your investment account statement to hand.

2. Open the account register.

3. Select the investment account covered by the investment account statement.

4. Select a transaction which corresponds to one of those appearing on your statement.

5. Right-click and select **Mark As**, then **Reconciled**. The transaction is now reconciled. The letter R will be shown in the transaction clearing field.

6. Repeat the clearing operation for all prices shown on your investment account statement.

In the event of any discrepancy between the transactions recorded in the account register and those shown on your account statement, edit the investment transactions accordingly.

The account balancing function is not available for balancing investment accounts.

Hour 8

Loans

THE CONTENTS FOR THIS HOUR

- The loan account

This hour consists of a single section which explains how to create and manage loan accounts.

THE LOAN ACCOUNT

The loan account is principally designed for monitoring loans, so that you can:

- monitor sums of money borrowed or lent;
- keep track of instalment due dates, so that you remember to enter your loan repayments;
- monitor payments made or received;
- be aware of the number of payments outstanding;
- see the amount of capital repaid, interest and miscellaneous charges (penalties for late payments, postage charges, insurance, etc.); and

- pass on any interest charges to your tax return if these are partially deductible (e.g. mortgage loans).

You might also create a loan account if you have lent someone a sum of money and they are repaying you more or less regularly – for example, a loan you have made to a friend or a member of your family.

Loan accounts are also applicable to agreed direct debits against purchases made by credit card.

Creating a loan account

Before you begin, have your loan papers to hand. Establish the significant details of the loan, such as the sum originally borrowed, frequency of repayments, interest rate, size of monthly instalments, etc.

1. On the menu bar, click on **Accounts**.

2. Click on **New Account**.

3. Indicate the name of the bank and click on **Next**.

4. Select **Loan** from the list of account types (see Figure 8.1). Click on **Next**.

5. Take note of the instructions shown and then click on **Next**. Money 98 will ask whether you are Borrowing Money or Lending Money. Select one of the two options and click on **Next**.

6. Enter a name for the loan and specify the lending institution. Click on **Next**.

7. Select one of the two options, **Adjustable Rate Loan** or **Fixed Rate Loan**. Click on **Next**.

8. Specify whether any payments have already been made. The answer will be Yes if you are creating a loan account based on an agreement already in progress. Personal contributions and guarantee deposits do not count as payments to be deducted from the amount loaned. Click on **Next**.

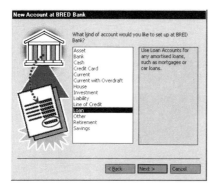

Figure 8.1: Selecting Loan for the account type

9. Enter the due date for the loan, i.e. the date on which payment must be made or will be debited from your spending account. Click on **Next** twice.

10. Specify the frequency of repayments and then click on **Next**.

11. Specify the basis for calculating interest on the loan. Click on **Next**.

12. Enter the loan amount, the annual interest rate, the duration of the loan, the principal plus interest, and the amount due at the end of the loan. If you do not know a value, e.g. capital plus interest, leave the field blank. Money 98 will calculate this value on the basis of the other information you supply. A summary of the loan conditions will then be displayed in a window (see Figure 8.2).

13. If you are satisfied that the loan conditions are correct, click on **Next**. If the conditions are wrong, click on **Back** and then change any conditions which appear to be incorrect.

14. Once you have clicked on **Next** in the summary window, you must create a category (here, named House Bills) and a subcategory (here, named Mortgage Interest) (see Figure 8.3). Click on **Next**.

Figure 8.2: Summary of loan conditions

Figure 8.3: Determining the categories associated with the loan

15. Specify whether or not the loan is a house mortgage. If so, click on **Yes** and then **Next**.

16. Specify whether the interest on the loan is tax-deductible. You should check with your lender for confirmation on this point. Click on **Next**.

17. Specify whether any other fees are associated with the loan, e.g. insurance premiums, solicitor's fees, etc. (see Figure 8.4). Enter the category, description and amount for each type of expense. Click on **Next**.

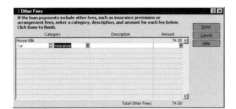

Figure 8.4: Entering details of any other fees

18. Enter the next payment due date and the account to be debited (see Figure 8.5).

Figure 8.5: Entering the next payment due date and the account to be debited

19. Money 98 displays a summary of the conditions applicable to the loan account (see Figure 8.6). Click on **Back** if you want to make any changes. Otherwise, click on **Next**.

20. Money now asks whether you want to associate the loan with an asset. In the case of a loan intended for the purchase of a property or a car, you should answer Yes.

21. Next, enter a name for the purchase if the loan concerned is a property mortgage, as well as the date of purchase. The value of the asset corresponds to the purchase price. Click on **End**.

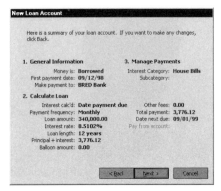

Figure 8.6: Loan account summary

Money 98 has just created two accounts. The first is the loan account itself, and the second is the associated asset account. The loan has been added to the Bill Calendar, which you can check by clicking on **Bills**. All scheduled payments corresponding to the loan will be taken into consideration in the loan account. According to the confirmation of any payments on the loan account, information about all such payments will be shown in the details for transactions associated with the loan account, in particular the capital and interest figures on each payment date (see Figure 8.7).

Date	Pmt Num	Payee	Payment	Principal	Balance
09/12/98	1	BRED Bank	3,776.12	340,000.00	336,223.88

You Owe: -£336,223.66

Figure 8.7: Display of capital and interest elements in a loan account

The details entered when you create a loan account should correspond to those appearing on the actual loan papers. Loan simulations can be carried out only with Money 98 Financial Suite.

Entering loan payments

If you have followed the above steps, all scheduled payments associated with the loan account will be shown in the Bill Calendar. As long as you confirm each payment as it is made, it will be updated in the loan account register.

However, if you have created a loan account involving variable or irregular payments – for example, in the case of money loaned to a friend or a member of your family – you will need to enter transactions directly into the loan account. In this case, proceed in the same way as for entering a transaction in a spending account.

Displaying and printing the amortisation report

To view all scheduled payments associated with a loan, you can display or print the amortisation table as follows:

1. On the menu bar, click on **Reports**.

2. Click on **What I Owe**.

3. Click on **Loan Amortization**.

4. Click on **Go To Report/Chart** at the bottom of the screen. The amortisation table will be displayed (see Figure 8.8).

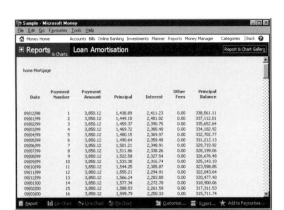

Figure 8.8: Amortisation table

5. To print the list of scheduled payments, click on **File** on the toolbar, followed by **Print**. Select the number of pages you want to print.

Hour 9

Cash flow management

THE CONTENTS FOR THIS HOUR

- Overview
- Setting up a budget

In this hour, we will see how to plan a budget. This will help you to pay your debts, organise your savings, minimise the impact of unforeseen expenses and so on.

OVERVIEW

To access the Budget function, click on **Planner** on the menu bar, and then on **Make a Budget & Savings Plan**. This will take you to the **Budget management** window (see Figure 9.1).

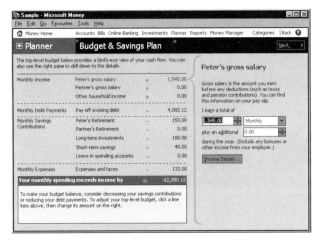

Figure 9.1: Budget management window

The **Budget & Savings Plan** window takes the form of a summary of your cash flow. This is an overview modelled on your financial situation, and should be as close as possible to reality in terms of the savings options, and yet remain flexible.

The conventional approach, as far as savings are concerned, consists of calculating available savings on the basis of the difference between income and expenditure. The Money 98 Budget function uses a different approach: the sum available is calculated on the basis of the income from which the various repayments and savings are deducted.

The aim of this simulation is to balance your budget.

- If the budget figure is close to zero, your budget is balanced. You have entered good estimates for the various elements of your expenses and savings.

- If the budget shows a surplus, you can use the difference for paying debts or for savings.

- If the budget figure is negative, you must reduce your expenses, debt payments or savings according to what your situation allows.

SETTING UP A BUDGET

As you will have immediately noticed on the Budget & Savings Plan form, the parameters to be managed are relatively few in number. This is because the budget is only an estimate which enables you to define guidelines on the basis of an actual situation and a forecast situation.

You can retrieve various categories of income and expenses, as follows:

- salary: your own and that of your partner, and any other household income;
- monthly debt payments;
- monthly savings contributions; and
- monthly expenses.

The aim is to reach a point at which a positive value is displayed in the small box showing the state of your budget. This box represents a collection of details you have given Money 98. Do not be tempted to bend the truth when you enter data, but try to remain objective.

Monthly income

This is the first budget heading you should complete. It covers your own salary and that of your partner, and any other household income. To fill in this item, select the line showing your own gross salary:

1. Click once on the line of the budget in which you want to enter details.

2. On the right of the screen, a vertical bracket contains the relevant entry fields. Enter your total monthly income, and

include any occasional bonuses by dividing them into monthly fractions.

3. Specify the frequency of your salary payments. For most salaries, this will be monthly (see Figure 9.2).

Figure 9.2: Fields for entering salary total and payment frequency

4. Click on **Income Details** to review any data you have already entered about your income (see Figure 9.3).

Figure 9.3: Income Details window

For the transactions entered in account registers, class your income and expenses according to categories. These categories are in turn divided into groups, and these are the budget groups which you partially retrieve into the Goal Planner, along with details of your income and expenses.

When you view the details for a budget item (e.g. Income Details in Figure 9.3), the left part of the window takes account of all items of income entered since the start of the accounting year. The figures shown are calculated by Money 98 on the basis of the data you have entered. For example, if you have entered a variable salary, Money 98 will calculate an average monthly salary based on the entered data. The more accounting data you enter, the more accurate will be the figures provided to help you set up your budget.

Using the **Income Details** window, you can take account of your regular monthly income without considering any occasional income, or you can spread this occasional income by giving it a monthly value. Thus:

- An end-of-year bonus can be entered as occasional income. This type of income is received. You can increase the monthly salary amount by one-twelfth of the value of the bonus.

- An unforeseen windfall, such as an inheritance, is also occasional income. However, since this type of income is not repeated year after year, do not incorporate it as monthly income.

In estimating your income and expenses, Money 98 also takes account of data entered in the Bill Calendar and any loan and investment accounts. However, it is up to you to decide the monthly amounts to enter in the budget: all Money 98 does is collate your data.

Monthly debt payments

In this part of the budget, enter all debts repaid in monthly instalments, such as mortgages and credit card balances (see Figure 9.4).

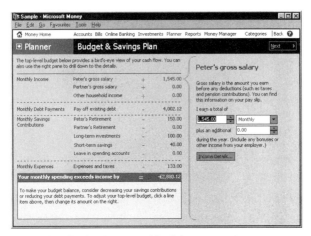

Figure 9.4: Budgeting monthly debt payments

Monthly savings contributions

In this part of the budget, enter all savings expenditure, such as:

- your pension and that of your partner;
- long-term investments;
- short-term savings; and
- spending accounts.

When entering pension scheme payments, express the amount as either an absolute value or as a percentage of your salary. You can also add any occasional payments made by your employer (see Figure 9.5).

The **Long-term investments** field is for any savings you put away for distant projects, e.g. savings accounts for accommodation.

The **Short-term savings field** is for money deposited in instant access savings accounts, for example, or any other form of savings which is immediately available in the event of any temporary financial difficulty.

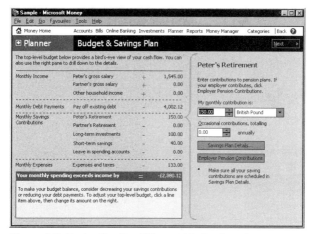

Figure 9.5: Budgeting for different kinds of savings

The **Spending accounts** field is for all unused money remaining in your account. Even if the amounts concerned may vary during the course of the year, estimate the average monthly value if this is more than zero.

Monthly expenses

In this part of the budget, enter figures for your monthly expenses excluding taxes, and the monthly taxes themselves in two separate fields (see Figure 9.6).

The average monthly value of expenses can be calculated automatically by Money 98:

1. Beside the **Monthly Expenses** field (right of the screen), click on **Expense Details**.

2. At the bottom of the **Expense Details** window, click on **AutoBudget** (see Figure 9.7). Money 98 will propose an average value.

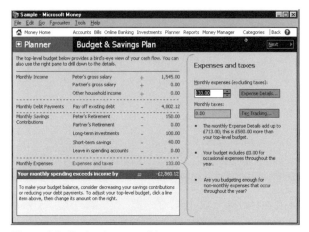

Figure 9.6: Budgeting monthly expenses

Figure 9.7: Expense Details window

3. Click on **Close**. Money 98 will offer to incorporate the average value in the budget. You can accept this offer, since the value can be freely changed at any time during your regular monitoring of this budget model.

Monitoring of tax sums should be carried out on the basis of your tax return for the previous year. Whatever method of payment you choose, enter the total amount of all taxes demanded from you and divide this figure by twelve.

In the **Budget** window, Money 98 displays a box advising any adjustments to your budget. Whenever you make any adjustments to your budget, check the text shown in this box, as it offers suggestions to help you achieve a balanced budget.

Hour 10

Online banking services

THE CONTENTS FOR THIS HOUR

- Available online banking services
- Access to online banking services

In the age of direct banking, banks have realised that it is in their interest to provide access to online banking services. Not only are these services available at all times, but they also make it possible to conduct transactions in real time. In this hour, we will explore some of the aspects of these online services which can be used via Money 98.

AVAILABLE ONLINE BANKING SERVICES

Online banking services are a set of free or charged services which are accessible by means of a simple telephone call or other form of remote communication.

- **Telephone banking.** These services are accessible by means of an ordinary telephone with a touch-tone keypad. When you call this type of service, you are connected to a recorded message which gives you step-by-step instructions on how to carry out certain operations such as obtaining account balances, requesting information, etc.

- **Internet services.** These services are accessible worldwide, via any Internet service provider (see Figure 10.1). If you expect to conduct transactions on a regular basis, you should contact your bank, who will tell you whether they provide online banking services via the Internet. If it does not, your request (very probably along with other similar enquiries) will force it to consider making such services available, since other competing institutions are setting up Internet banking services at a rapid pace.

Figure 10.1: Information page for a bank accessible via the Internet

Hardware

You must have a modem capable of communicating over the telephone network. Some systems may use special media, e.g. ADSL, cable networks, satellite link, etc.

- **Internal modem.** This is a card which plugs into an expansion slot inside the computer. This card is integral to the machine, and cannot be removed for use with a laptop.

- **External modem.** All models currently sold operate at around 56 Kbps. Up until now, there have always been two competing technologies, the X2 and K56, although the V.90 protocol has become more and more standard. You will no longer find any modems operating at lower speeds except on the second-hand market. External modems offer the advantage of portability, which makes them particularly useful for carrying out transactions using a laptop.

- **Cable and ADSL connections.** Both these forms of connection require a special type of modem. ADSL and cable modems provide only Internet access. While the fastest ordinary telephone modems are limited to a speed of 56 Kbps, a cable connection is capable of downloading at over 300 Kbps and an ADSL connection at 2 Mbps.

The last two of these are new technologies. ADSL has the advantage of being installed on existing telephone lines, in other words with no additional wiring. A filter keeps the analogue channel separate from transmissions on the digital channel. You can even make or receive telephone calls during digital transmissions. The two types of communication do not interfere with each other.

Software

The modems currently available on the market are supplied with software drivers and various utility programs, and often include subscription offers for connection to the Internet.

Money 98 is capable of accessing the various online services without the use of an external program. However, the following is a list of all the programs you will need to make the most of your modem:

- a fax transmission/reception program;

- an Internet browser program; and

- an e-mail program.

If you do not yet have a modem or are not yet subscribing to an Internet service provider, see Appendix 1 for a list of ISPs.

ACCESS TO ONLINE BANKING SERVICES

You will not be able to gain access to online services using only the instructions in this book. The wide variety of procedures and conditions of use mean that you will have to proceed in several stages.

Subscribing to online banking services

To gain access to online banking services, you will need to take out a subscription with your bank. To do this:

1. Contact your bank and ask for full information about available online services, including details of the software which can be used and the costs of accessing these services.

2. If you are happy with the stipulated conditions, apply for your access code and password.

3. Test the services available via the Internet to familiarise yourself with the procedures.

4. Launch Money 98 and click on **Online Banking** on the menu bar. The screen should then appear as shown in Figure 10.2.

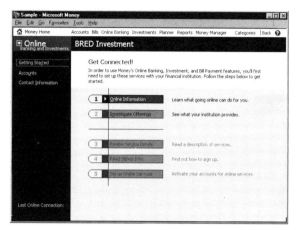

Figure 10.2: Online Banking access screen

5. Click on **Online Banking** on the left of the screen and select the account for which you want to configure access to online services.

6. Configure online services for this account, using the installation files supplied by Money 98.

You are liable for all telephone charges and all costs associated with accessing your bank's online services.

Once you have set up the correct configuration, you are ready to carry out online transactions.

▆▆▆▆ Online banking services

Money 98 provides access to various online services:

- **Online Statements.** You will no longer need to check your bank statements manually. You will also be kept informed of your account balances.

- **Online Bill Payment.** Pay your bills from your computer. (Not all banks offer this service.)

- **Online Quotes.** Update the prices of your investments. This service is free, and does not require a subscription to your bank's online services. For more information, see Hour 7: Updating prices automatically.

- **Access to the Money Web site.** Information, discussion forum, etc.

- **Microsoft Technical Support.** Access to the Microsoft Money Technical Support page.

Downloading a statement

Here is the procedure for downloading a bank statement using online banking services:

1. On the menu bar, click on **Online Banking**.

2. Select the account for which you want to use an online service.

3. Click on **Connection** (at the left side of the screen).

4. Click on the online banking operation you want to carry out, then confirm by clicking on **Connect**.

5. Money 98 will activate the modem, dial the network access number, and then send the code for access to your banking institution's server.

6. Follow the on-screen commands to navigate to the account statement screen. To update your account, click on the appropriate button. Transactions are processed line by line, with a confirmation request for each line of the account statement as it is processed. If necessary, add any additional information.

With Money 98, you are not restricted to consulting information about your bank accounts. You have access to other services as well.

Hour 11

Miscellaneous operations

THE CONTENTS FOR THIS HOUR

- Invoices
- Importing and exporting accounts
- Restricting access to your accounts

INVOICES

Money 98 contains an invoicing module to simplify the issuing of invoices. This will be particularly appreciated by those using Money 98 for professional purposes.

The invoicing module allows you to draw up invoices, quotations and pro-forma invoices. These can be printed on your own letterhead or on standard A4 paper (210 × 297 mm). VAT will be recorded automatically, and the invoice will be allocated to the appropriate category.

▰▰▰▰ Initialising the invoicing module

Before you can use the invoicing module, it must be initialised.

1. Click on **Tools** on the Money 98 function bar (see Figure 11.1).
   The invoicing module window will be displayed (see
   Figure 11.2).

Figure 11.1: Starting the invoicing module

Figure 11.2: The appearance of the invoicing module

2. Click on **Company Setup** (lower left of the screen).

3. Enter your company details (see Figure 11.3). Most of these
   elements will be carried over on to the invoice itself, including
   your VAT number. Confirm your details by clicking on **OK**.
   If you make a mistake or any of your details change, enter
   new details for your company.

Figure 11.3: Defining your company details

Entering a client

Creating a list of clients will enable you to quickly retrieve a given client's details and incorporate them in your invoices.

1. In the invoicing module window, click on **Customer View** (upper left of the screen).

2. Click on **New Customer** and enter the relevant details (see Figure 11.4). If you subsequently need to modify any of the details entered, all you have to do is return to this list of clients, select the client card to be modified, and click on **Edit**.

Figure 11.4: Entering details on a client card

▬▬▬ Entering a product

Products include not only the items you sell, but also various types of services. Entering products will enable you to save time when you compile your invoices.

1. In the invoicing module window, click on **Item View** (upper left of the screen).

2. Click on **New Item** and enter the relevant details (see Figure 11.5). Any card associated with an article can subsequently be modified by clicking on **Edit**.

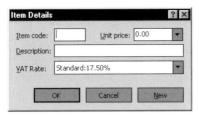

Figure 11.5: Entering the details of an item

Money 98 enters a default VAT of 17.5%. There are other rates applicable to highly specialised products or associated with certain tax regulations on imports; if you need to use any special VAT rates, you can configure them by clicking on **VAT Rate View** in the invoicing module window.

In the **Unit price** field of the **Item Details** window, enter the pre-tax value of the product. If you only have the tax-inclusive price to hand, proceed as follows to enter the pre-tax value based on the tax-inclusive figure.

1. Click on the arrow to the right of the **Unit price** field.

2. Click on the calculator and convert the tax-inclusive price to a pre-tax price (see Figure 11.6).

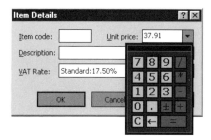

Figure 11.6: Using the calculator when entering a pre-tax value

Proceed as follows to convert a tax-inclusive price to a pre-tax price:

- For a tax-inclusive price which includes VAT at 17.5%, divide by 1.175. Example: £40.00 / 1.175 = £34.04 exc. taxes.

 Conversion is carried out to five decimal places. In the other direction of conversion – i.e. when compiling the invoice – the conversion of a pre-tax price to a tax-inclusive price may result in a difference due to the rounding methods used in calculations.

If you have numerous items for which you need to convert tax-inclusive prices to pre-tax prices, it is better to use a pocket calculator. All calculators include a "constant operation" function. Use this function as follows:

1. Switch on the calculator.

2. As a precaution, press the **C** (Clear) key twice.

3. Enter the second element of the operation and press the operator key twice. For example, to repeat the operation of dividing a tax-inclusive price by 1.175, you would enter 1.175 and then press the / key twice. This will program the operation "divided by 1.175" as a constant operation.

4. Now enter the tax-inclusive price to be converted and press the = key. The pre-tax price will be shown.

5. Convert another tax-inclusive price by entering the tax-inclusive figure and then pressing the = key.

These instructions on how to use a calculator may seem unnecessary, but the calculator incorporated in Money 98 does not include this "constant operation" function.

This will save you the trouble of endlessly re-keying conversion calculations. With a calculator programmed for constant operation and your product list to hand, you will be able to enter all tax-inclusive prices from your catalogue in the Money 98 invoicing module quickly and accurately.

Creating an invoice

This function is not fully operational until you have entered your company details and references for your clients and products.

1. In the invoicing module window, select **Form View**.

2. Click on the **New Form** button at the bottom of the screen. The invoice form will be displayed (see Figure 11.7).

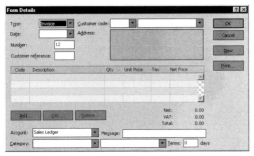

Figure 11.7: Invoice form

3. For our purposes, select **Invoice** as the transaction type.

4. Complete the other fields. If you fill in a field for which you have no record, Money 98 will inform you that it has no corresponding records and will invite you to create them. Accept this offer if the invoice concerns new clients or new articles.

5. Once you have entered all relevant details on the invoice, click on **OK**.

Invoices can be associated with a spending account. For the sake of simplicity, you can create a special invoicing account.

You can print any invoice by selecting it in the invoicing module window and clicking on **Print**.

If you make a mistake in the compilation of an invoice, you can easily modify it as long as it has not been added to the corresponding account.

Once an invoice has been incorporated in an account, no further modifications can be made to it.

1. In the invoicing module window, select **Form View**.

2. Select the invoice to be incorporated in the account.

3. Click on **Add To Account**. The invoice will be integrated with the account shown in the **Account** field of the invoice form.

An invoice which has been confirmed as belonging to a particular account can no longer be modified using the invoice form. However, it can be partially modified by clicking on **Edit** in the Account Register.

IMPORTING AND EXPORTING ACCOUNTS

The import/export function allows you to exchange data with other financial management programs.

Importing files

The file import function enables you to incorporate files and accounts in the following formats: QIF (Quicken), QUI, QDT/QDB, OFC (for exchanging banking data) and OFX. The last two formats are specific to the exchange of banking data. Ask your bank what options are available for the exchange of banking data.

If an imported file contains information already entered in Money 98, this information will be duplicated.

To import data contained in a Quicken file, you should first familiarise yourself with the Help topic entitled Quicken Conversion Overview.

1. On the menu bar, click on **File**.

2. Select **Import** (see Figure 11.8).

Figure 11.8: Selecting the Import function

3. Select the file to be imported and confirm by clicking on the **Import** button.

4. Select the account in which you want to place the imported data. Follow the instructions displayed.

▬▬▬ Exporting files

To export data from an account, proceed as you would for importing data, but select the **Export** option.

Money 98 will export the entire file contents as a new file in QIF (Quicken) format. However, category and subcategory names should be kept short (less than 15 characters) since long names may not be compatible with other applications.

Remember that you can also export reports in the form of text files where each field is separated by a tab character. These files can be imported into most spreadsheet and word processing programs, as well as tax return software.

RESTRICTING ACCESS TO YOUR ACCOUNTS

Your accounts may contain confidential data (such as names of clients, lists of contacts, etc.), or you may not want to risk any errors being generated by allowing anyone else to enter accounting transactions. In this case, you can restrict access to the file by using a password.

1. On the menu bar, click on **File**.

2. Select **Password**.

3. Type the password (see Figure 11.9).

Use a password that is easy for you to remember but hard for other people to guess. You can use a maximum of 16 characters.

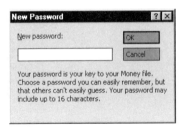

Figure 11.9: Entering a new password

Do not write your password down anywhere near your work station, or in a computer file. If this file were to be destroyed, it would be far more difficult to recover than if you had written your password down on paper.

The password is associated with an individual file. If you change files, the second file can be opened without a password. If you send someone a password-protected file, the recipient will need this password in order to open the file.

Hour 12

From the pound to the euro

THE CONTENTS FOR THIS HOUR

- Creating an account managed in euros
- Entering transactions in euros
- Compiling reports
- Entering transactions in a foreign currency
- From the pound to the euro

Everyone is talking about the euro, and many people are worried about having to manage this new currency. The accounts managed by Money 98 can only handle one currency at a time, but this chapter offers a solution to help you with this accounting changeover.

Just as it did for the previous generation in the change to decimalisation, it will undoubtedly take you a while to get used to the euro. The euro is now a currency you can use for your bank payments, even though coins and notes in euro denominations are still unfamiliar and require mental converting. Using Money 98 and a little account manipulation, you can enter your income and expenses in both currencies, pounds and euros, and view the overall balance expressed in the currency which is more familiar to you.

CREATING AN ACCOUNT MANAGED IN EUROS

Once the euro is officially in place, you may receive an invoice made out in euros. You will have to pay this invoice in euros. In order to account for this invoice in its original currency, you will need to create a spending account which is managed in parallel with your initial spending account, but which handles transactions conducted in euros.

Begin by creating a second spending account, as follows:

1. To create a new spending account to handle euros, double-click on **Accounts** on the navigation bar. The screen will show a list of the accounts used in the current file.

2. Click on **New Account** in the lower right-hand part of the **Account Manager** window.

3. Create a new account with the same parameters as your initial spending account. When you arrive at the window requesting the balance of the new account, enter a balance of zero.

4. Select the euro as the new currency from the list offered (see Figure 12.1). In the following examples, we have set the exchange rate as 1.43 euros to the pound.

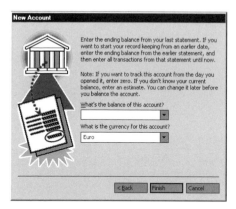

Figure 12.1: Entering the balance and the working currency for the new account managed in euros

ENTERING TRANSACTIONS IN EUROS

Let us imagine that you have just written your first cheque made out in euros. You have just put stamps worth 25.41 euros on some parcels; the post office accepts payment in this new currency, you have written a cheque in euros, and in due course your bank statement will show a debit for the same amount.

Now you need to enter this transaction. You have two possible approaches:

- Enter the transaction in the spending account managed in pounds sterling. When you come to enter the amount, all you need to do is press **F8**, enter the amount in euros, and specify the euro and its exchange rate (see Figure 12.2). Once you have confirmed the amount entered in euros, the equivalent sum in pounds will be shown in the **Amount** field – in this case £17.79, which corresponds to 25.41 euros.

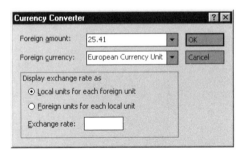

Figure 12.2: The window activated by the F8 key, in order to convert a transaction not expressed in pounds

- Enter this transaction in the spending account managed in euros. In our example, we have entered a single transaction corresponding to the payment of 25.41 euros made at the post office (see Figure 12.3).

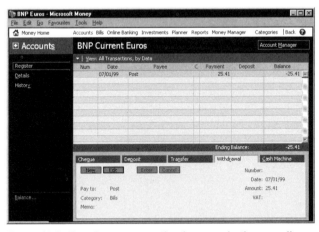

Figure 12.3: Entering a transaction in euros in the spending account managed in euros

By managing payments made in euros in a separate account, you will be able to view the amounts involved in these transactions in the form in which they are expressed on the associated paperwork. Using our example, it is easy to check the consistency of our management of the dual-currency account (see Figure 12.4).

If we calculate the difference between the balance of the account managed in pounds and the overall balance of all accounts, we arrive at a figure of £17.79, which corresponds to the sum of 25.41 euros converted into pounds (see Figure 12.4).

Figure 12.4: The balance of accounts is consistent

COMPILING REPORTS

When you compile reports, all sums expressed in foreign currencies are converted into pounds sterling. You can easily check the accuracy of this conversion.

1. Select the **Reports** option on the Money 98 navigation bar.

2. Select **Where the Money Goes** from the list of available reports.

3. Click on **Go to Report/Chart** in the bottom left. The display should be similar to the one shown in Figure 12.5.

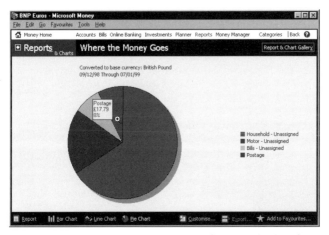

Figure 12.5: Report on Where the Money Goes, in pie-chart form

When this report is displayed, all you have to do is position the mouse cursor over any sector to open a small information window. Place the cursor over the smallest coloured sector and the information window will show the payee as the post office and the amount as £17.79. This correctly equates to the sum originally entered in euros and converted into pounds.

You will find the same consistency of accounting for the euro in all other reports. The report shown in Figure 12.6 is obtained by clicking on **Reports** on the navigation bar, then selecting **Spending Habits** from the list of report types on the left. Now click on **Income vs. Spending** in the central part of the screen.

In our accounting model – simplified for the purposes of illustration – we see once again that a sum entered in euros has been accounted for in pounds.

Converted to base currency: British Pound
09/12/98 Through 07/01/99

Category	Total
Expense Categories	
Bills	17.79
Household	154.00
Motor	43.40
Postage	17.79
Expense - Unassigned	0.00
Total Expense Categories	232.98
Grand Total	-232.98

Figure 12.6: On the report of Income vs. Spending, amounts entered in euros are converted into pounds

ENTERING TRANSACTIONS IN A FOREIGN CURRENCY

Some banking institutions already accept occasional cheques made out in currencies other than pounds sterling. If you only carry out this type of transaction infrequently, there is no need to create a special account for the management of the currency concerned.

Holders of post office cheque accounts can issue cheques made out in any of the main European currencies provided the payee also has an account with a post office or similar institution (e.g. GiroBank).

For example, to pay 350 Norwegian kroner to the Norwegian National Veterinary Service, which has a post office account, all you need to do is make out a post office cheque in the usual way and write NOK after the amount, i.e. 350 NOK.

To enter a foreign currency debit transaction in the spending account, proceed in the same way as for entering a transaction conducted in pounds:

1. Click on **Accounts** on the navigation bar.

2. Select the spending account concerned.

3. In the transaction form (lower part of the screen), click on **Cheque** and then begin entering the various payment details.

4. When you come to enter the amount, press **F8**. This will open a window for entering the amount in a foreign currency.

5. In this foreign currency window, enter the amount and then select the currency used (Norwegian kroner, for example). Next, specify that the exchange rate should be displayed as local units for each foreign unit (see Figure 12.7).

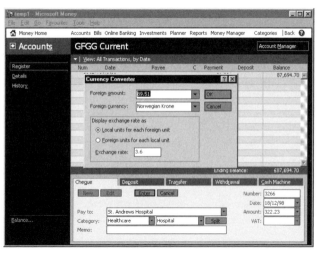

Figure 12.7: Entering a foreign currency payment in an account managed in pounds

6. Complete the entry by clicking on **OK**. In the **Amount** field on the transaction form, the sum should be shown converted into pounds.

When you receive your account statement, check that the amount debited matches your calculations. If it does not, adjust the amount by modifying the exchange rate. If the banking institution has charged commission or other additional fees, allocate these transactions to the relevant categories. Exchange commission and transfer charges would be placed in the **Bank Charges** category. If necessary, create an **Exchange Charges** subcategory.

Before making a payment in a foreign currency using your cheque book, it is essential that you check with the institution managing the account to ensure that this operation is permissible. You should also find out what fees will be charged. Some banking institutions have quite high minimum charges. It is therefore worthwhile checking up on the various procedures for making payments in foreign currencies, the time taken for funds to be cleared, the fees charged, the acceptability of the cheques concerned in the target country, etc.

FROM THE POUND TO THE EURO

Whether we are for or against it, the euro is an irreversible change to which we are committed, and one which we will have to learn to get used to. You can start getting to grips with the transition right now with the help of Money 98. The following are the various stages involved in making this transition.

Now that it has been officially announced that the euro can be used for making and receiving payments, create one or more accounts to duplicate those currently managed in pounds sterling.

1. Enter all transactions conducted in euros in these accounts managed in euros.

2. Be prepared to close those accounts managed in pounds once there are no further transactions being entered in them.

3. Carry over the balances of any closed accounts managed in pounds to the accounts managed in euros, after converting these closed account balances into euros.

4. When most or all of your accounts are managed in euros, click on **Tools** and then **Options** on the menu bar.

5. In the **Options** window, click on the **Currencies** tab and select the euro as the currency to be used. Check the exchange rate, and make any adjustment if necessary (see Figure 12.8).

6. Click on **Set Base Currency**. A warning window will appear (see Figure 12.9). Confirm the change of base currency by clicking on **Yes**. Money 98 will shut down, as indicated in the warning window.

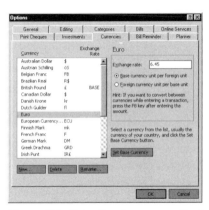

Figure 12.8: Selecting the euro as the base currency and setting the exchange rate

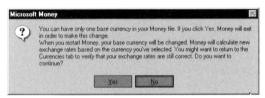

Figure 12.9: Clicking on Yes in the warning window will confirm the euro as your base accounting currency

From now on, whenever you start Money 98, all transactions entered will automatically be accounted for in euros. If there are still any unclosed accounts managed in pounds, you can continue to enter transactions conducted in pounds in these accounts.

Using our model as an example, when you click on **Accounts** on the navigation bar you will see a screen showing the balance of each account and the overall balance for all accounts. Naturally, the individual balances of accounts, whether managed in pounds or euros, remain unchanged. Only the overall balance is modified. When Money 98 used the pound as the base currency, this balance was £1,610.22. Now that the base currency is the euro, it stands at 1,127.15 euros (see Figure 12.10).

Now that the euro has been officially declared to be a valid currency for banking transactions, its exchange rate has been established. According to the agreements reached between the countries adopting the euro, rates of exchange between the various European currencies should no longer fluctuate.

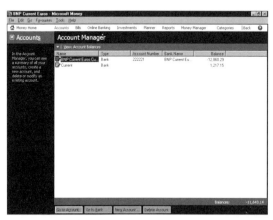

Figure 12.10: Once Money 98 is using the euro as the base currency, the overall balance will be displayed in euros

Once the base currency has been changed – in other words, when the time comes to switch from the pound to the euro – it is easy to check the consistency of the accounting data compiled by Money 98.

Click on **Reports** on the Money 98 navigation bar, then on **Spending Habits** and **Income vs. Spending**. You should see a report similar to the one shown in Figure 12.6, in which amounts entered in British pounds have been converted into euros (see Figure 12.11). In our example, the amounts previously entered in euros in the accounts managed in euros remain unchanged.

Converted to base currency: Euro
09/12/98 Through 07/01/99

Category	Total
Expense Categories	
Bills	25.41
Household	220.00
Motor	62.00
Postage	25.41
Expense - Unassigned	0.00
Total Expense Categories	332.82
Grand Total	-332.82

Figure 12.11: In the report on Income vs. Spending, amounts entered in pounds are converted into euros

In conclusion, Money 98 is perfectly suited to the management of accounts in euros. If you follow the advice given in this chapter, you will have no problem handling two currencies during the transitional phase. Although the euro will take some time getting used to, there is nothing to stop you continuing to use pounds as your base currency, even if all your accounts are managed in euros. If you choose to do this, reports will be compiled in pounds.

Appendix

Online information

ABOUT THIS APPENDIX

In recent years, it has become possible to find financial and stock-market information from the Internet. Numerous sites offer rapid and detailed information, some of which is provided free of charge (apart from telephone charges and a subscription to an Internet service provider).

If you have cause to consult stock-market, legal or other information on a regular basis, and you do not have access to the Internet, we recommend that you take out a subscription to an Internet service provider. Many providers now offer unlimited access in return for a very reasonable monthly subscription fee.

TELEPHONE

It is possible to search for UK business addresses on the Intenet. One useful site is:

http://www.ukonline.co.uk/ukonline/directory.html

Or try the Yellow Pages online:

http://www.yell.co.uk/

NEWSGROUPS

Newsgroups can be accessed using a compatible browser program. Recent browsers can access these groups without difficulty.

news:microsoft.public.money

INTERNET SITES

The Internet sites listed below have all been checked, and the links are valid at the time of writing. Most of these sites belong to large companies and government bodies. Consequently, the addresses are unlikely to have been changed. If a link appears not to work, we suggest you try to connect again, entering only the root of the address. For example, if you find you cannot connect to the address:

http://www.microsoft.com/money/

you can omit the last part of the address and try connecting again to:

http://www.microsoft.com/

If no part of the address works, there are various possible explanations:

- The server is too busy. Try again later.

- The server is out of order. Try again later.

- The server is overloaded. Try again later.

- The server has moved. Make a note of the new link.

- The server has been closed down. Delete the link from the list.

In the time between the compilation of this book and its publication, new services will have become available. In addition to the list offered here, you should also try using search engines to find other resources. If you do not know how to use search engines, another book in this series covers this subject: *A Simple Guide to Searching the Internet*. All sites are in English only unless stated otherwise.

Money 98 help and information

MICROSOFT. The Microsoft information site. Product information, links to other information and technical support sites, hints and tips:

http://www.microsoft.com/money/

MSN MONEYCENTRAL. The Microsoft financial information site. Access to online quotes and headings including investment, retirement & wills, taxes, real estate, etc.

http://moneycentral.com/

Calculators

MONEYADVISOR. Links to various sites offering programs for calculating loans, investment yield, retirement savings, maximum loan amount, interest rates, redemption values, net worth, consumer price index, mortgage rates, etc.

http://www.MoneyAdvisor.com/

THE SYNDICATE. Javascript bond calculator.

> **http://www.moneypages.com/syndicate/bondcalc.htm**

NUMAWEB. Calculators for options, multi-options, warrants and convertible bonds.

> **http://www.numa.com/**

News services

REUTERS. The famous press agency online. Wide range of information on finance, politics, economics.

> **http://www.reuters.com/**

YAHOO NEWS. Economic information. Access to other information (politics, society, etc.).

> **http://www.yahoo.com/**

Taxation & fiscal affairs

EUROPA. European Union server: Parliament, Council, Commission, Court of Justice, Court of Auditors and other European Union (EU) bodies. In all languages of the European Union.

> **http://europa.eu.int/**

HM TREASURY. Run by the UK Treasury. Texts of all laws, decrees, announcements on taxation, the euro, excise duty, consumption, the Budget, competition, etc.

> **http://www.hm-treasury.gov.uk/**

The UK Government website for the Euro:

> **http://www.euro.gov.uk/**

Financial glossaries

INTERNATIONAL FINANCIAL ENCYCLOPAEDIA. The international encyclopaedia of finance. Very useful if you visit English-speaking Internet sites. Gives definitions of all financial terms and abbreviations.

> **http://www.euro.net/innovation/Finance_Base/ Fin_encyc.html**

TERM FINANCE. Undoubtedly one of the most comprehensive online glossaries. Gives clear definitions of the principal terms used in the stock market and financial trading. Accessible in several languages: English, French, German and Italian. Very useful to small-scale speculators looking for information on the Internet to gain a better understanding of foreign stock-market terminology.

> **http://www.finance.wat.ch/termfinance/**

Stock market information

BELFOX Belgian Futures & Options Exchange. Stock-market information on Belgian and international securities quoted on the Belgian market. Site in English, French and Dutch.

> **http://www.belfox.be**

BLOOMBERG. Access to financial information from the principal American and world financial centres. Bloomberg is a privately-owned financial information TV channel.

> **http://www.bloomberg.com/**

If you have the Real Player plug-in installed on your browser, you can view Bloomberg's TV broadcasts at the following address:

> **http://www.bloomberg.com/videos/top/live.ram**

The Bloomberg channel is also available via satellite.

CBOT Chicago Board Of Trade. Information on the Chicago stock market.

> **http://www.cbot.com**

CME Chicago Mercantile Exchange. Stock-market information on commercial securities traded on the Chicago exchange.

> **http://www.cme.com**

DB Deutsche Börse *[German stock market].* Information on securities traded on the German market. In English and German.

> **www.exchange.de**

GOLD EAGLE. Comprehensive information on quoted prices for gold and derivative materials. Some useful links to databases showing the trends of financial market indices over a period of almost a hundred years.

> **http://www.gold-eagle.com/**

HKFE Hong Kong Futures Exchange. Stock-market information on securities quoted on the Hong Kong exchange (see Figure A.1).

> **http://www.hkfe.com**

Figure A.1: Home page of the Hong Kong Futures Exchange website

ITALIAN Stock Exchange. All prices quoted on the Italian market (see Figure A.2).

http://www.borsaitalia.it/

Figure A.2: Home page of the Italian Stock Exchange website

LIFFE London International Financial Futures and Options Exchange. Stock market information on British securities.

http://www.liffe.com

London Stock Exchange. Information on the exchange and news.

http://www.londonstockex.co.uk

MONEP Marché des Options Négociables de Paris *[Paris Negotiable Options Market]*. MONEP began trading on 10 September 1987. It is regulated by the Conseil des Marchés Financiers [Financial Markets Council] (CMF) and run by MONEP SA, a subsidiary of SBF-Bourse de Paris.

http://www.monep.fr/english/defaultuk.html

MONEY NET. Access to prices – free with a certain time-lag, or in real time for subscribers.

http://www.moneynet.com/

NASDAQ. Specialist site for Nasdaq securities. Fast display of prices and graphs.

> http://www.nasdaq.com/

NYMEX New York Mercantile Exchange. New York stock market information.

> http://www.nymex.com

PR-LINE. Graphs for all RM securities, intra-day or greater, comparisons between graphs. Free access. In French.

> http://www.prline.com/

La Bourse de Paris SBF *[Paris Stock Exchange].* Quotations for securities in the CAC40, SBF120 and 250 and the Secondary Market Index, latest published financial information, half-hourly updates on Paris stock market indices, member companies, information on the various departments of SBF, calendar of events, introductions on to the Secondary Market, Bours'Info, etc. (see Figure A.3).

> http://www.bourse-de-paris.fr/defaulgb.htm

Figure A.3: Home page of the SBF Bourse de Paris website

SFE Sydney Futures Exchange. The Sydney stock-market information page.

> **http://www.sfe.com.au**

SICOVAM. Sicovam SA is the central French depositary, and manages the payment and delivery systems (Relit, RGV).

> **http://www.sicovam.com/us**

SIMEX Singapore International Monetary Exchange. Singapore stock market information.

> **http://www.simex.com.sg**

SOFFEX & SWX Suisse. The Swiss stock market (Swiss Exchange, SWX) regulates the organisation and operation of the financial markets. The SWX is the only stock market in the world with entirely computerised trading and clearing. In English, French and German.

> **http://www.bourse.ch**

SWISS QUOTE. Free direct access to prices for the principal Swiss securities (Nestlé, ABB, Swissair, Roche, etc.). Access quotes by code or by name. Allows direct retrieval of the greatest fluctuations in the day's trading, and the largest volumes traded.

> **http://www.swissquote.ch/**

TIFFE Tokyo International Financial Futures Exchange. Tokyo stock market information (see Figure A.4). In English and Japanese.

> **http://www.tiffe.or.jp/**

Figure A.4: Home page of the TIFFE website

TSE Tokyo Stock Exchange. Tokyo stock exchange site. In English and Japanese.

http://www.tse.or.jp

Wall Street City. For those interested in the American markets. This site allows you to follow various items of news, create portfolios or view graphs.

http://www.wallstreetcity.com/

WOQATS. Real-time and delayed American (NYSE, Nasdaq, Amex) and European (London, Paris, Frankfurt, Xetra, Zurich) stock market prices, financial news, analyses. Access to certain areas restricted to subscribers. In English and French.

http://www.woqats.com/

YAHOO FINANCE. Access to prices using a simple Sicovam code (fifteen minutes for shares, real-time for indices). Prices cross-referred with currencies. Free access.

> **http://quote.yahoo.com/**

Newspapers and media

The list of media websites provided below includes only those which offer stock market and/or economic information.

BBC News. Financial website of the BBC. Business news, daily London market data, FTSE data updated every half hour.

> **http://news.bbc.co.uk/hi/english/business/**

Financial Times. Website of the *Financial Times* newspaper . Synopses of articles in recent editions, including the current edition. Today's news, world news, special reports, etc.

> **http://www.ft.com/**

Guardian Unlimited. Website of the *Guardian* newspaper. Some financial and business news, archived news. Free to use but you need to register.

> **http://www.guardianunlimited.co.uk/**

Financial Markets Daily. Daily newspaper covering the fixed income and equity markets. Subscription cost.

> **http://www.fmdaily.qpg.com/**

CNNFN. The CNN financial network. Latest news, personal finance, world business, travel, markets, etc. Free access.

> **http://www.cnnfn.com/**

Wall Street Journal. Interactive edition of the US financial journal. Subscription cost, although at time of writing there is a free 2 week trial period for online subscribers.

> **http://www.wsj.com/**

The Economist. Website of the magazine *The Economist.*

> **http://www.economist.com/**

Laws and decrees

The list of websites offered below contains only the sites of official bodies which provide comprehensive information.

European Court of Justice. Report on activities, publications, press releases.

> **http://europa.eu.int/cj/en/index.htm**

EUROPARL. Multilingual information website covering the activities of the European parliament and its constituent bodies and political groups.

> **http://www.europarl.eu.int/**

Home Office. Home page for the UK Home Office. Information on UK internal affairs: press releases, publications, legal affairs, etc.

> **http://www.homeoffice.gov.uk/**

UK Treasury. Home page for the UK Treasury.

> **http://www.hm-treasury.gov.uk/**

Sarrebruck Legal Web. French-German legal centre, legal resources and University of la Sarre. Introduction to German public law. Distribution list for circulation of public data on the Internet. Karlsruhe agreement on transnational co-operation. Bilingual legal resources (French Constitution of 1958, fundamental law of the German Federal Republic). In French and German. Partial information in English and Japanese.

> http://www.jura.uni-sb.de/france/

Search engines

Yellow Pages. Free access to its databases to locate a company anywhere in England by its fax or telephone number, or website address.

> http://www.yell.co.uk/

Miscellaneous services

Bank of England. Offers news and documentation on recent financial issues, plus the changeover to the euro, the bank itself (history, role, organisation), the UK banking system, detailed information about the functions of the Bank of England.

> http://www.bankofengland.co.uk/

Bourse Novice. A server to initiate you into the workings of the stock market.

> http://www.bourse-novice.com/

ESI. Electronic share information. Information on companies and shares taken from many different sources. Buy and sell UK listed shares. Look up company news, analytical information and forecasts. Paid service.

> http://www.esi.co.uk/

Finance Net. A springboard to everything on the Web to do with finance. Over 2,500 sites categorised by subject and by country. Online quotes, stock market advice, interactive discussion forum on the stock market and financial markets, and numerous useful headings.

http://www.finance-net.com

Patrimoine Management & Technologies *[Asset Management & Technologies].* Services for professionals involved in financial management for individuals. In English, French and Spanish.

http://www.patrimoine.com/

Department of Trade and Industry. News and support for UK business and industry.

http://www.dti.gov.uk/

The Share Centre. Investment advice service.

http://www.share.co.uk

Stockwiz. Program to help investors find investment opportunities. Runs under Windows 95 and NT 4.0.

http://www.stockwiz.com

Walmaster. Technical analysis software site. Dictionary of technical analysis terms, with examples. Very well done.

http://www.walmaster.com

Statistics

CIA – Central Intelligence Agency. Official site of the CIA, the American government service. Direct access to the World Factbook 97. All social, political, economic and geographic data, with maps, for all countries of the world. Commentaries on political and economic stability. An essential tool if you are planning commercial relations or investments in a foreign country.

http://www.odci.gov/cia/publications/factbook/ country-frame.html

INSEE. Website of *l'Institut National de la Statistique et des Etudes Economiques [National Institute for Statistics and Economic Studies]*. Headings: press releases about new publications, population and density of communes at the time of the 1990 census, information, etc. In French and partially in English.

> **http://www.insee.fr/**

OECD. Access to socio-economic data on the countries involved in the OECD, covering numerous subjects: education, health, safety, agriculture, industry, transport, etc. Highly detailed reports available free of charge.

> **http://www.oecd.org/statlist.htm**

PWT The Penn World Tables. Access to socio-economic documents on 152 countries and 29 subjects.

> **http://arcadia.chass.utoronto.ca/pwt/**

Strategic Road. Access to essential social, economic and political data on most countries of the world. Numerous documents taken from the renowned CIA World Factbook 97. Type of information: general data, news, economy, analysis and summaries, economic strategy, business information, etc. In English and French.

> **http://www.strategic-road.com**

UCL IRES Institut de Recherches Economiques et Sociales *[Institute of Economic and Social Research]*. Catholic University of Louvain (Belgium). Access to Belgian and European economic statistics. Access granted after free subscription. In English and French. Link to Norwegian socio-economic statistics (in English and Norwegian).

> **http://www.econ.ucl.ac.be/IRES/STAT_IRES.html**

Index

F

H

I

L

M